Challenging Mathematics

A selection of secondary school mathematics problems

Edited by Peter Giblin and Ian Porteous

Mathematical Education on Merseyside

Oxford University Press 1990

Oxford University Press, Walton Street, Oxford OX2 6DP

Oxford New York Toronto
Delhi Bombay Calcutta Madras Karachi
Petaling Jaya Singapore Hong Kong Tokyo
Nairobi Dar es Salaam Cape Town
Melbourne Auckland

and associated companies in
Berlin Ibadan

Oxford is a trade mark of Oxford University Press

© Mathematical Education on Merseyside 1990

ISBN 0 19 914361 7

Note on photocopying

The puzzle pages of this book are designed for photocopying, but each page may be reproduced for class use **only** within the purchaser's school or college.

Text designed and typeset by Gecko Ltd.
Printed in Great Britain

Preface

The problems and puzzles in this book were all set between 1978 and 1989 in a CHALLENGE competition for first and second formers in secondary schools in and around Merseyside. The competition, which is still running, attracts about 3500 entries each year, is sponsored by local industry and commerce and is one of the activities organized by Mathematical Education on Merseyside. MEM, which is run from the mathematics departments of Liverpool University, brings together teachers and enthusiasts from all branches of post-primary education in a combined effort to make mathematics more relevant and more fun for youngsters at school.

The organisers of CHALLENGE have always striven to prevent the competition becoming elitist, let alone a mini-olympiad, so that about half the problems set each year have been, we hope, accessible to a very wide ability range. It is, nevertheless, a competition, so questions are included each year the purpose of which is to sort out the best in the age-group. Thus there is material here which can challenge the mathematical ingenuity of children beyond the age of $13½$ which is the cut-off for entering the competition. Some more is said about the style of questions in the Introduction.

In a competition with 3500 entries any ambiguity in a question will cause it to be misread by someone! Needless to say, we do not have a perfect record here; for this edition we have tried hard to remove any remaining doubtful wordings. We have also removed a couple of downright mistakes: on one occasion a question which should have had four answers had, through incorrect wording, several thousand answers and to our embarrassment some entrants tried to list them all!

The inspiration for the questions comes, naturally, from a wide reading of the puzzle and problem literature as well as from the subconscious minds of the setters. There are, however, very few chestnuts here, and there are (we think!) a number of truly original ideas. The setters have, in any case, always tried to put questions in an amusing or practical context. The only editing, besides the removal of ambiguities and errors, has been in questions which are 'dated'. CHALLENGE is an annual competition, so it is natural to include questions relevant to the number of the year (such as using the fact that 1987 is a sum of two squares in a particular way). These questions have been for the most part retained, but with altered wording to fit with the new format. CHALLENGE has been sponsored over the years by a number of organizations, and the names of one or two have crept into the questions. We hope that the other sponsors will not feel in any way slighted.

Finally, a few words about the CHALLENGE competition itself. It consists of two rounds, six questions per round, and each round is tackled over a weekend during the Spring Term. All scripts are marked – help with this mammoth task comes from teachers, lecturers and also students at the University. A prize-giving evening takes place in May at Liverpool University where prize-winners, mums and dads, and sometimes whole families, come to what we provocatively describe as 'an evening of mathematical recreation'. That such activities as mathematics and recreation can coexist is no surprise to the prize-winners, but it comes as a shock to some of the guests. We hope that the shock is a pleasant one.

Peter J. Giblin (Chairman, MEM)
Ian R. Porteous (President, MEM)
Liverpool, November 1989

Introduction

The questions are arranged in four Parts according to difficulty (see below). The harder problems (Part 3 onwards) should be suitable for third and fourth form pupils and the open-ended questions (Part 4) are essentially project work. Little technical knowledge is assumed, though simple algebra can turn what would otherwise be trial-and-error into something more systematic. We have tried to indicate in the solutions how these more systematic methods can be used, and in the solutions to the open-ended questions we have often taken the subject matter well beyond the explicit material of the question to aid with investigations.

The grouping of questions in fives is to provide a variety of subject-matter and style, keeping to roughly the same order of difficulty within each group. Of course the judgement of difficulty is subjective, but we hope that the division proves useful. Here is a description of the contents of the various Parts.

Part 1: 'Easy'. Straightforward tangram-type questions; straightforward enumerations, possibly involving a simple deduction; simple uses of logical reasoning; pure arithmetic or simple applications to length, weight, etc.; jokes.

Part 2: 'Middling'. Slightly harder tangram-type questions; somewhat trickier enumeration problems, or optimization ('what is the shortest route?' etc.), where it is an advantage to be systematic; slightly harder logical deductions; numerical questions where being systematic avoids a lot of work; questions where elementary algebra can be an advantage (but isn't crucial); questions needing enumeration followed by deduction; arithmetic of fractions; speed, angles, ratios; very simple three-dimensional problems.

Part 3: 'Challenging'. Tricky enumerations; harder arithmetic problems, where it is not so obvious what to do or where some process has to be carried out many times; questions where a fair amount of understanding is required before you can begin, perhaps involving logical thought; questions where some algebra is needed; harder geometrical questions in 2 or 3 dimensions.

Part 4: 'Open-ended questions'. The first eight or so are mainly numerical while the others have a geometrical flavour, stronger in some than in others. The questions are not necessarily inherently difficult (though some are) but there is a clear possibility of developing the topic further. This is made explicit in the question and in the solution.

In terms of the Attainment Targets of the National Curriculum, all of AT1 to AT6, dealing with number and the beginnings of algebra, are represented here, except that we do not explicitly use the manipulation of inequalities. Graphical representation (in AT7) is not used either, though there are a few places where it could be used in a 'more advanced' understanding of what the question is about. AT9 and AT10 are well-represented and there is some elementary data handling (AT12), usually in deciding which of various options satisfies some criterion of optimality. There is nothing about probability. The Levels of Attainment (1 to 10) will of course vary considerably. Roughly speaking through the first three Parts of the book the level will rise from 3 (or even 2) to 7 or 8. Part 4 is more investigative and the level nearer the high end (7 or 8) with, in the open-ended parts of questions, the possibility of even higher levels being called on. We hope that the solutions will make this clear in any individual case.

Acknowledgements

CHALLENGE has been sponsored for several years by Royal Insurance, who have not only provided all the money for prizes but have also done the printing. The other sponsors of Mathematical Education on Merseyside, past and present, are:

Deloitte, Haskins and Sells (Chartered Accountants)
GEC Plessey Telecommunications Ltd
Imperial Chemical Industries (Chemicals and Polymers Group)
London Mathematical Society
National Westminster Bank plc
Ocean Transport and Trading plc
Pilkington plc
Royal Bank of Scotland plc
Shell U.K. Ltd
William M. Mercer Fraser Ltd (Actuaries and Consultants)

It will be obvious to anyone looking through this book that a special debt is owed to the artist, Peter Ackerley of ICI in Runcorn, who has exactly caught the spirit of the CHALLENGE competition.

Finally we want to thank all the people – teachers, lecturers, students and others – who have contributed their time and effort to the production of the CHALLENGE competitions since 1978.

P.J.G.
I.R.P.

Contents

Preface 3

Introduction 4

Acknowledgements 5

The puzzles (bracketed page numbers refer to solutions)

Part 1 'Easy'

1a	I's down	9	(55)
1b	Ice across	9	(55)
1c	Wholesum	9	(55)
1d	Correct!	9	(55)
1e	Where Alfred failed	10	(55)
2a	A powerful start	10	(56)
2b	L-ish	10	(56)
2c	Joinery	10	(56)
2d	Age-old problem	11	(56)
2e	Appropriate steps	11	(56)
3a	Initial challenge	11	(56)
3b	4L = L	11	(57)
3c	Drawn and quartered	12	(57)
3d	Food for thought	12	(57)
3e	Mixed up	12	(57)
4a	Fit the first	12	(57)
4b	Fit the second	13	(57)
4c	Genesis	13	(57)
4d	Cross number puzzle	13	(58)
4e	La petite locomotive	13	(58)
5a	Starters	14	(58)
5b	Tangram	14	(58)
5c	Odd arrangements	14	(59)
5d	Down on the farm	15	(59)
5e	Standing orders	15	(59)

Part 2 'Middling'

1a	Lick this!	16	(60)
1b	Garden of the year	16	(60)
1c	Ferret this out!	16	(60)
1d	Wherehouse?	17	(60)
1e	Time for a swim	17	(61)
2a	One good turn	18	(61)
2b	Figure it out	18	(61)
2c	A scratch calculation	18	(61)
2d	Pentagran	18	(62)
2e	Penalty decision	19	(62)
3a	Matchboxes	19	(62)
3b	Sell out	19	(62)
3c	Key products	20	(63)
3d	Gloppits	20	(63)
3e	Cattle grid	20	(64)
4a	Pentominoes	21	(64)
4b	Child's play	21	(64)
4c	Oh boy!	21	(65)
4d	Bread line	22	(65)
4e	Great little escapes	22	(65)
5a	Scenic route	22	(65)
5b	Fair squares	23	(65)
5c	More from less	23	(65)
5d	Put-up job	23	(66)
5e	Mr M. Y. Opia	24	(66)
6a	Four-minute kilometre	24	(66)
6b	Cubicles	24	(66)
6c	Going, going, gone!	25	(67)
6d	Hobson's ices	25	(67)
6e	Vandalised stones	25	(67)
7a	Starthere	26	(67)
7b	Booksale	26	(68)
7c	Break block	26	(68)
7d	Birthday girls	26	(68)
7e	Island magic	27	(68)
8a	Belt up	27	(69)
8b	Logic	27	(69)
8c	Beast of burden	28	(69)
8d	Second rate	28	(69)
8e	Plan for redundancy	28	(69)
9a	The right times	29	(70)
9b	Super shell	29	(70)
9c	Annelid vs Gastropod	29	(70)
9d	Mr Compost	30	(70)
9e	Team work	30	(71)
10a	Insurance angle	30	(71)
10b	Grannie's secret	31	(71)
10c	Best friend	31	(71)
10d	Space invaders	31	(72)
10e	Postal order	32	(72)

Part 3 'Challenging'

1a	Magic it!	33	(73)
1b	Presents a problem	33	(73)
1c	It's a knockout	33	(73)
1d	Busy bees	33	(73)
1e	Revolutionary	34	(74)
2a	Chimps are champs	34	(74)
2b	Insecticide	35	(74)
2c	Coggly	35	(74)
2d	Twice two	35	(75)
2e	Final challenge	36	(75)
3a	Plot plants	36	(75)
3b	Square routes	36	(76)
3c	Dig this	37	(76)
3d	Counter feat	37	(76)
3e	Drink problem	38	(76)
4a	Davy Jones's locker	38	(77)
4b	Raffle Baffler	38	(77)
4c	Rooms with a view	38	(77)
4d	Adverse conditions	39	(78)
4e	Escalation	39	(78)
5a	Plotting and planning	39	(78)
5b	Four square	40	(78)
5c	Sum how	40	(79)
5d	Cartography	40	(79)
5e	On the cards	41	(79)
6a	Job opportunities	41	(79)
6b	Close encounters	42	(80)
6c	Across the board	42	(80)
6d	Wrap up	42	(80)
6e	Wind band	43	(81)
7a	Fair play	43	(81)
7b	Sextuplets	43	(81)
7c	Metric rules	44	(81)
7d	Hic!	44	(82)
7e	Acid test	45	(82)
8a	Mark this	45	(82)
8b	Ball points	45	(82)
8c	Anathematics	46	(83)
8d	Cube routes	46	(83)
8e	The last one	46	(84)

Part 4 'Open-ended'

1	Chain reaction	47	(85)
2	Downhill all the way	47	(86)
3	$+ = \times$	48	(87)
4	Power cuts	48	(88)
5	Spadework	48	(88)
6	Cornered	49	(89)
7	Grinding away	49	(90)
8	Countdown	49	(90)
9	Arc light	50	(91)
10	Mower time	50	(91)
11	Slipped disc	50	(92)
12	Circle line	51	(92)
13	New circle line	51	(93)
14	Let's face it	51	(94)
15	Valhalla	52	(94)
16	Damp course	52	(95)
17	Night at the round table	53	(95)
18	Fearsome foursome	53	(95)
19	Space men	54	(96)
20	Gemini	54	(96)

1a I'S DOWN

Show how to put eight blocks this shape down on the board on the right, so as to cover all the squares except the centre square.
(You are allowed to turn the blocks round.)

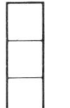

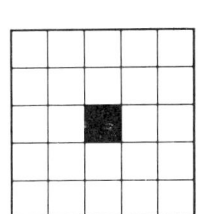

1b ICE ACROSS

Ken the Baker has just enough icing for a 1 cm thick layer across the top of a square cake 30 cm × 30 cm.
He makes several rectangular cakes 12 cm × 20 cm instead, and wants to put a ½ cm thick layer of icing across the top of each of these.
How many of the smaller cakes can he ice?

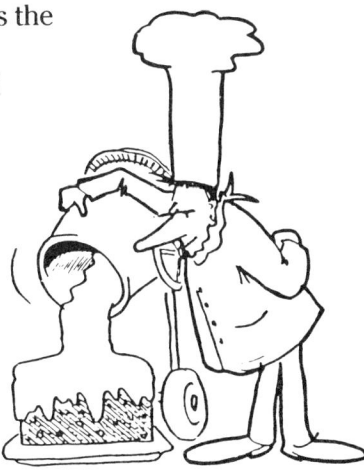

1c WHOLESUM

Three whole numbers when added together make 10.
When multiplied together they make 30.
What are the numbers?

1d CORRECT!

This sum is wrong.
Change just one of the nine figures so as to make it correct.

```
  1 2 3
+ 2 9 7
───────
= 3 3 0
```

1e WHERE ALFRED FAILED

When placed in the proper order and completed, the following are the instructions for baking a cake.
According to the recipe, the baking time is about twenty-five minutes from the time when the cake is put into the hot oven. However, as Alfred found to his cost, one has in practice to be careful not to burn the cake!

Write out the full instruction for success. The ingredients are:

1. Take cake out of oven
2. Return to step ....
3. Switch off the oven
4. Wait 5 minutes
5. Wait 20 minutes
6. Wait 30 minutes
7. Put the cake in the oven
8. Is the cake cooked?
9. Switch on the oven
10. If yes, proceed to step ..... but, if no, to step .....

2a A POWERFUL START

Find whole numbers n and m such that

$$2^n - 2^m = 1984$$

[$2^3 = 2 \times 2 \times 2 = 8$, $2^4 = 2 \times 2 \times 2 \times 2 = 16$, and so on.]

2b L-ISH

Show how to cover the shape on the right with six L-shaped tiles like this.

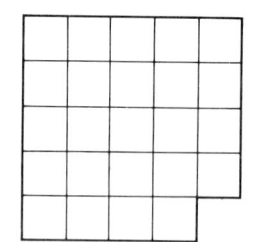

2c JOINERY

Can you assemble this window frame from these four pieces?

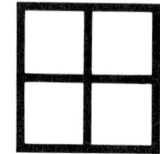

2d AGE-OLD PROBLEM

In ten years time the combined age of two brothers and two sisters will be 100.
What will it be in five years time?

2e APPROPRIATE STEPS

A heavy ladder can be moved by 'walking' it – keeping it nearly vertical and pivoting it first around one foot and then around the other.
The ladder leans in an almost vertical position against a wall, with its feet on two spots on the ground.
What is the least number of steps needed to 'walk' the ladder round so that its feet are on the spots opposite to where they began?

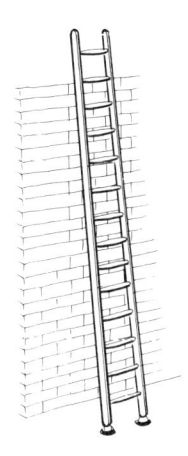

3a INITIAL CHALLENGE

Clues Across
1. The number of seconds in half an hour, three minutes and one second
4. The largest whole number that goes exactly into 60 and 75
6. The nearest whole number to 7.32×8.7
8. (3 down $\times$ 4 across $- 2$) $\times$ 7

Clues Down
1. A prime number with equal digits
2. A multiple of 6
3. $\sqrt{361}$
5. A multiple of 9
7. A square number

3b 4L = L

Fit together four pieces this shape to make a piece twice as large but with the same shape.

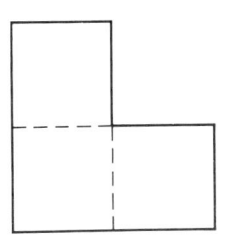

3c DRAWN AND QUARTERED

Here is another 'tan-gram' question.
Fit together four pieces this shape (a square and half a square) to make a piece twice as large but with the same shape.

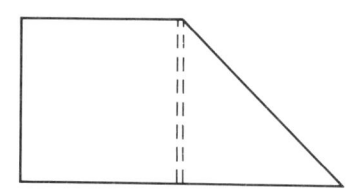

3d FOOD FOR THOUGHT

How much should be charged for Egg & Mash?

MENU.
EGG & CHIPS.   150p.
SAUSAGE & CHIPS 180p.
SAUSAGE & MASH. 135p.

3e MIXED UP

'Watson! Whatever will these villains get up to next? Here are three bottles of poison which I found at the scene of the crime, the first labelled Cyanide, the second labelled Arsenic and the third labelled Cyanide and Arsenic – a mixture!
'I happen to know that the three labels are correct but that they have been cunningly stuck on so that every label is on the wrong bottle.'
Watson sniffed at the bottles. 'Holmes, the first bottle smells of cyanide!'
Which bottle contains what?

4a FIT THE FIRST

How many pieces of this size and shape

will fit (without overlapping) into this shape?

4b FIT THE SECOND

Find a shape made up of four squares stuck together which will fit exactly four times (without overlapping) into this shape.

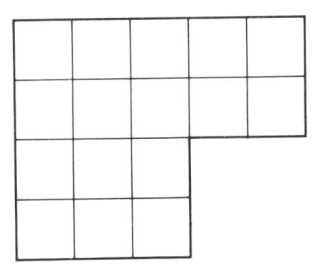

4c GENESIS

When I say two numbers, Adam adds them and Eve multiplies them.

If Adam's answer is 10 and Eve's is 16, what are the two numbers?

If Adam's answer is 15 and Eve's is 56, what are the two numbers?

Finally, what are the two numbers if Adam says 31 and Eve says 210?

4d CROSS NUMBER PUZZLE

Solve this puzzle given that the figures to be entered in the four squares are all different from each other.

Across: 1. A number divisible by 5
         3. A number divisible by 7
Down: 1. A number divisible by 12
        2. A number divisible by 13

4e LA PETITE LOCOMOTIVE

Not so many years ago some tins of cocoa in France carried a picture of this engine to make the product more attractive to children.
What is curious about a go-ahead company using this illustration?

5a STARTERS

(i) Find three consecutive whole numbers whose total is 42.

(ii) Three quarters of an hour ago it was as many minutes past 11 o'clock as it is now minutes to 12 o'clock.

What time is it?

5b TANGRAM

The diagram shows five shapes arranged to form a square.

By moving **one** of the shapes can you make the five form a triangle?

Again moving one shape can you make a parallelogram?

By rearranging the shapes in any way, can you make a Greek cross, like the one below?

Give your answers in the form of diagrams.

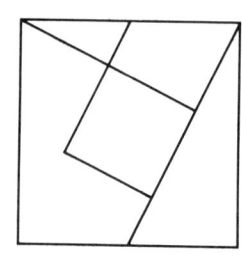

5c ODD ARRANGEMENTS

Using the numbers 1, 3, 5 and 7, the signs $+$, $-$, $\times$ and also brackets, we can make many numbers.
For instance, 4 can be made as $4 = 3 - 1 + 7 - 5$ and also as $4 = (3 - 1) \times (7 - 5)$.

Show how to make each of the numbers from 5 to 10 (inclusive) in this way.

Give just one way of making each number. Remember to use all of 1, 3, 5 and 7 each time.

5d DOWN ON THE FARM

A poultry farmer keeps only ducks and geese, which make feathers for eiderdowns, and he has equal numbers of the two birds.
Each duck is worth £9 and each goose is worth £11.
His total stock of birds is worth £10,000.
How many birds has he?

5e STANDING ORDERS

Fred and Hilda went shopping in Lewis's department store, and they got accidentally separated.
Hilda remembered that Fred had often told her that it was better, when two people were looking for one another, for one of them to stay in one place, while the other searched. So she stayed in the fabric department and waited.
But it didn't work. Why not?

1a LICK THIS!

In 1968, Malta issued a Christmas stamp shaped as in the scale drawing.
The stamps were issued to Post Offices in sheets of 60 with no waste except round the edges of the sheets. The perforations along the top and bottom of the sheets were also straight.

Show how this can be done – you need not draw all 60 stamps, but your drawing should make clear how the stamps could be arranged on the sheet.

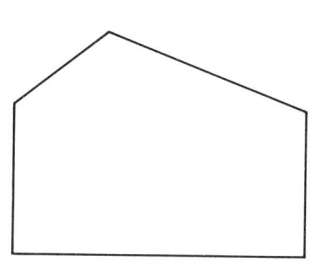

1b GARDEN OF THE YEAR

When I moved house in 1987, my garden had three square lawns. Each was a whole number of feet along a side.

Two lawns were the same area but the third was slightly smaller. The total area of grass was 1987 square feet.

What was the area of each lawn?

1c FERRET THIS OUT!

My father is four times as old as I am, and twelve times as old as the ferret.

How many times older than me was my father when I was as old as the ferret is now?

1d WHEREHOUSE?

The Kwikspend supermarket chain owns four shops along a road, as in the diagram, where the marks are at mile intervals along the road (so B is 4 miles from A, and so on).

A   B   C   D

Shop A requires 8 deliveries per week, shop B requires 4, shop C requires 7 and shop D requires 6. Each delivery is a full van-load and the transport cost is £3 per mile.

A warehouse is to be built at one of the sixteen mile markings, and deliveries will be made from it to all four shops.

Where should it be built to make the total weekly transport bill as low as possible?

Would the answer be any different if shop D required only 5 deliveries per week?

1e TIME FOR A SWIM

The diagram shows a plan of Maze City, USA. Some streets are more crowded than others, and my driving times, in minutes, along each section of street, are shown on the plan.

Which is my quickest route from home to the swimming pool, given that at each junction I go either North or East? (The time taken to make the turns may be neglected.)

Is there a quicker route if I can go any way at each junction?

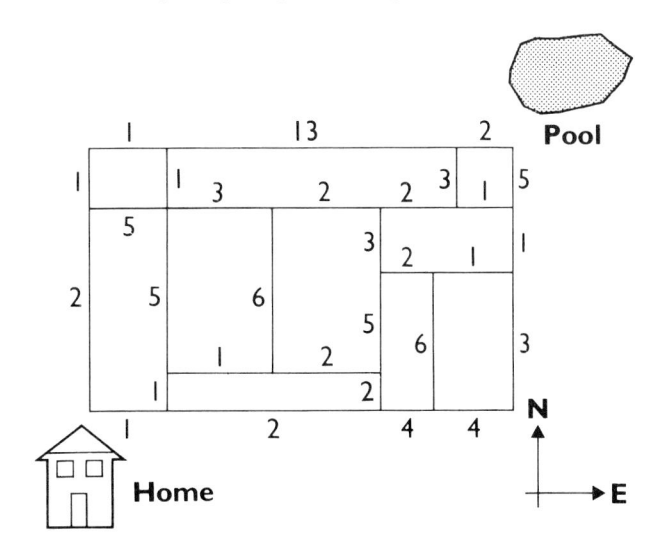

2a ONE GOOD TURN

The chain wheel of a bicycle has 52 teeth.
The sprocket attached to the hub of the back wheel has 13 teeth.
The circumference of the back wheel is 2.2 metres.
About how far does the bicycle travel when the pedals go round once?

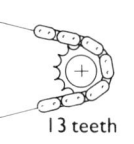

2b FIGURE IT OUT

Here are two ordinary addition sums, in which each of the letters A, B, and C stands for a figure from 1 to 9.
What is the number ABCB?

```
  A B C B         A A C C
+ B C B A       + C C A A
---------       ---------
  A A C C 0       9 9 9 9
```

2c A SCRATCH CALCULATION

Plastic fingernails cost 30 p each but, for orders over £10, you get one free for every ten you pay for. How much would 44 cost?
Is it possible to buy just 35?

2d PENTAGRAN

Five Senior Citizens, arriving late for Bingo, find that the only available seats are two in the front row and three in the row behind. In how many different ways can they seat themselves?

2e PENALTY DECISION

A furniture company hires five new joiners and wishes to give each of them one of five specific jobs.
So that their abilities may be compared each joiner provides a specimen of each task. The foreman awards each piece of work a number of 'penalty points' as shown in the table below. He intends to allocate the joiners to the jobs so that the total number of penalty points is as low as possible.
Who does each job?

TASK	JOINER A	B	C	D	E
V	2	7	8	5	7
W	6	4	7	6	8
X	4	2	5	6	2
Y	7	3	8	5	4
Z	6	5	6	4	7

3a MATCHBOXES

Three matchboxes of the same size can be made into a rectangular block in three different ways as shown in the diagram.
In how many ways can six matchboxes be made into a rectangular block?

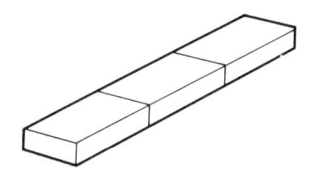

3b SELL OUT

Alice took charge of the Cake Stall at St. Monica's High School Spring Fair.
Her first customer bought a third of her cakes and the second bought a third of the remainder. Finally the third customer bought a third of the cakes left by the other two.
Alice's friend Joyce came by and said 'Don't forget to save me a dozen cakes as you promised'.
'Oh! I'm sorry I can't', said Alice. 'I've only eight left.'
How many cakes had Alice at first?

3c KEY PRODUCTS

The key to a code is given by three whole numbers.
The key is transmitted from headquarters by three agents each of whom is given the product of two of them. Suppose that the numbers transmitted are 432, 540, 720.

What is the key to the code?

3d GLOPPITS

A factory which makes 'Gloppits' is to be re-equipped. There are two types of machine available whose specifications are as follows:

Type	Cost	Daily output	No. of men per machine
1	£500	30 Gloppits	1
2	£1500	40 Gloppits	2

The Company does not wish to spend more than £40,000 on the machines and the factory can accommodate at most thirty machines and fifty men.

How many of each machine should be installed to give the greatest daily output and what would be the cost of the machines?

3e CATTLE GRID

A farmer has 41 cows and lives in a house surrounded by eight fields, three of which he can see from each window. There is one window in each wall of the house.
One day he noticed that he could see exactly 15 cows through each window and also he noticed that each field had one or other of two particular numbers of cows in it.

Find these two numbers and draw a diagram to show how the cows were arranged.

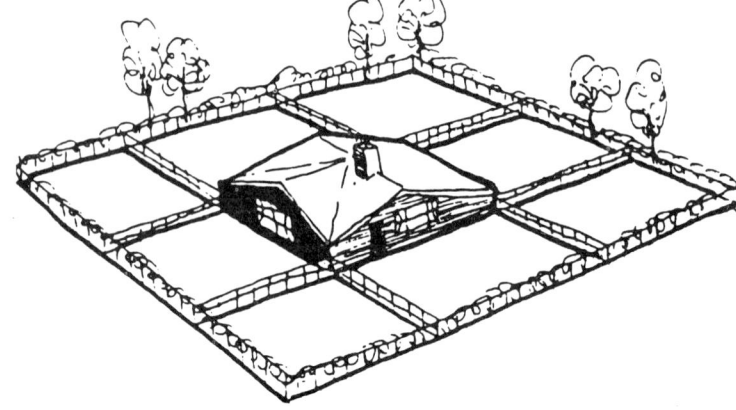

4a PENTOMINOES

With five small squares, all the same size, twelve different flat shapes can be made by sticking squares together along their sides. (By 'different' we mean that one shape cannot be turned round, or turned over, so that it looks exactly like another shape.)
Three of these shapes are shown here:

Can you find the other nine?

Jack has two pieces, like this:

Jill has two pieces, like this:

Which of the twelve shapes can Jack make with his two pieces?
Which can Jill make with her two?

4b CHILD'S PLAY

Two children found a block of stone with peculiar markings on it as shown in the picture.
They correctly decided that it was an ordinary addition sum, each of the three symbols representing a different number. They were surprised to find that, when they had got numbers to fit, each had a different addition sum.

Can you find both?

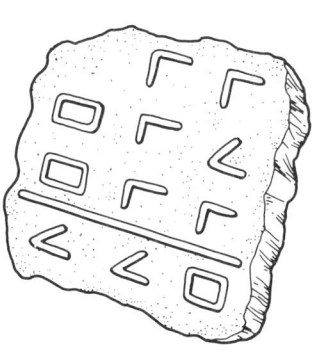

4c OH BOY!

Back in 1985 Bill and Brenda were Boy George fans and they each had a square photograph of their hero stuck on their bedroom wall. Each photograph was an exact whole number of centimetres along a side, but Brenda's was slightly bigger than Bill's.
When they added up the areas of their photographs they found, to their amazement, that the answer was exactly 1985 square centimetres!

What were the side-lengths, in centimetres, of the two photographs?

4d BREAD LINE

The diagram shows some of the streets of Crosstown.
The stars represent the positions of three baker's shops which are to be supplied from one bakery. This is to be positioned at a crossroads so that the sum of the distances along the streets from the bakery to the three shops is as small as possible.

Where should the bakery be sited?

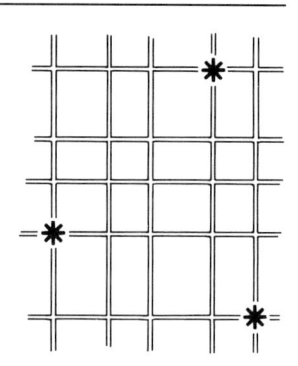

4e GREAT LITTLE ESCAPES

Intoxicated by deregulation, a bus company decides to run a service between Walton Gaol and Speke Airport in Liverpool. The route varies slightly in each direction so that the journey takes 35 minutes from Walton to Speke and 45 minutes from Speke to Walton.
Buses are to leave Walton at 9.00, 9.20, 9.40, etc.,
and Speke at 9.10, 9.30, 9.50, etc.
What is the least number of buses required to maintain the service, assuming there are no delays?
How long must the buses wait at each terminus between journeys?

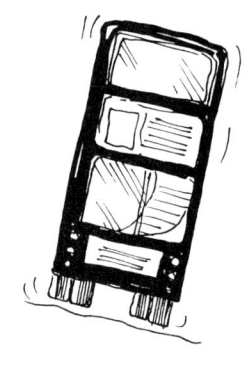

5a SCENIC ROUTE

Our map shows the road system on scenic Graph Island.
Design a route for the island's only coach that never crosses its own path but does take tourists along every stretch of road exactly once.

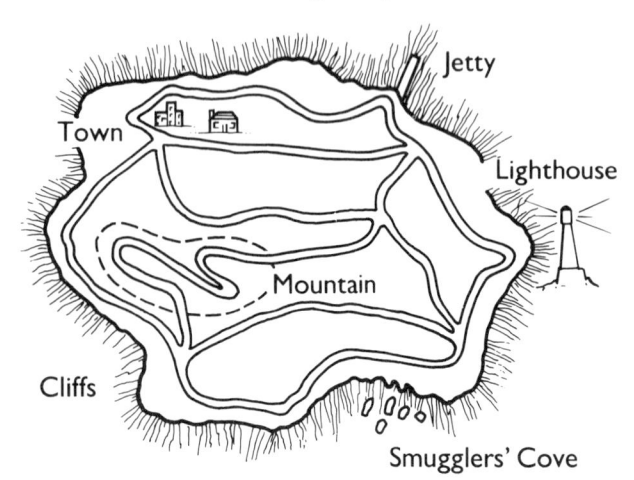

5b FAIR SQUARES

Sandra got a pile of 365 coloured tiles for Christmas with which she made patterns.
She quickly found that she could make two square patterns at the same time, one with 19 tiles along each side and the other a little two by two square made from the four tiles left over.
Some time later she was delighted to find two other squares that she could make simultaneously, with no tiles left over.

What sizes were these squares?

5c MORE FROM LESS

During half-term Sandra spent some time playing again with the coloured square tiles she got for Christmas. But some of the original 365 tiles had got mislaid. She cheered up when she found that now there were **three** different ways of making two square patterns at once, each time with no tiles left over.

How many tiles did she still have?

5d PUT-UP JOB

Three builders, Winclough, Barreys and Farretts, provide estimates for putting up three new buildings at a school. These are the gymnasium, the library and the dining hall. Each builder will construct **one** new building and the total cost is to be as low as possible.
Who should build what and what will the total cost be?
The table shows the estimates in thousands of pounds.

	Winclough	**Barreys**	**Farretts**
Gymnasium	48	48	44
Library	56	60	68
Dining hall	42	44	46

© OUP 1990. This page may be reproduced for class use within the purchaser's institute

5e MR M. Y. OPIA

Mr Opia has four letters to send but he has lost his glasses and manages to send each person someone else's letter.

How many ways are there of this happening?

6a FOUR-MINUTE KILOMETRE

A cyclist rides 600 m up a hill and 400 m down the other side. His speed is twice as fast downhill as uphill and the whole journey takes four minutes.

How long does it take him to reach the top?

6b CUBICLES

The Hotel Mathematicus is a thousand-room complex suitably close to Times Square. Max Factor wanted four rooms for his minions. 'Yes, I've got four rooms' said the receptionist, 'the room numbers are all perfect cubes and three of them add up to the fourth. Oh, and Room 1 is having some new units fitted, so you can't have that.'

Which rooms did Max Factor have?

(The first four cubes after 1 are 8, 27, 64, 125.)

6c GOING, GOING, GONE!

Mrs George-Henry, who owns a toy shop, decided to have an after-Christmas sale. She asked her daughter Lisa the following question.
'This doll costs £18. In the first week I'll sell it for half price. If it's not sold I'll take a third off for the second week, and if it's still not sold I'll take a sixth off for the third and final week. So, how much would it cost in the third week?'
Lisa replied: 'One, take away half, take away a third, take away a sixth, is nothing. So you'll be giving it away!'
Her mother laughed. 'I'm not that stupid,' she said.

Can you explain why Lisa was wrong, and find out how much the doll would really cost in the third week?

6d HOBSON'S ICES

Giuseppe Hobson sells ices; only cones, but with each cone you get two large scoopfuls, with twenty flavours to select from.

How many choices does that provide?

6e VANDALISED STONES

There used to be 90 stepping stones, one at every corner of each of the small squares in this array. But what with vandalism and government cuts the stones are in disrepair and only the ones drawn are left.

Jumping along a side of a small square, from one stone to another, is easy.
Jumping across a diagonal of a small square, from one stone to another, is harder and longer jumps than this are not possible.

What is the smallest number of harder jumps that you must do, in order to get from A to B?

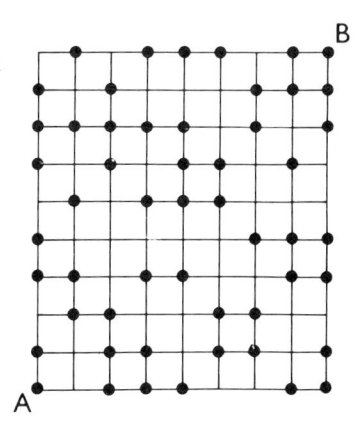

7a STARTHERE

There is a star!
It looks squint because it is squint.

What is the sum of the angles at its five points?

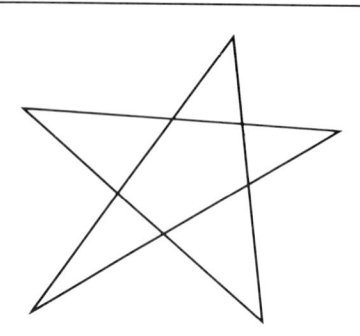

7b BOOKSALE

Twenty-five books on a bookshop shelf are arranged from left to right in increasing order of price, the difference in cost between adjacent books being 50p.
For the price of the most expensive book one could instead buy the book in the middle of the row and one of the two books next to it.

What would it cost to buy all the books?

7c BREAK BLOCK

A block of chocolate consists of twenty-four squares arranged in four rows of six.
It has to be broken into its twenty-four squares by clean straight breaks, each break making two pieces out of one.

What is the smallest number of breaks needed to do this?

7d BIRTHDAY GIRLS

Tina and Louise recently celebrated their birthdays on the same day.
Tina is now four times as old as Louise was when Tina was the same age as Louise is now.
Louise is a teenager.

How old are the two girls?

7e ISLAND MAGIC

A river has four islands joined to each other and to the banks by bridges as shown. On each island W there lives a Witch and on each island G there lives a Goblin.

Asses, Bears and Camels wish to cross from Westminster to Midland, but it is dangerous because:

1. A Witch, as is well known, always eats any Ass who arrives on her island.
2. A Goblin eats any Bear who arrives on his island.
3. A Witch will transform all Bears into Camels and all Camels into Bears before letting them leave her island.
4. A Goblin will transform all Asses into Camels and all Camels into Asses before letting them leave his island.
5. No bridge may be crossed twice by any creature, even if it has been turned into something else.

What animals might be observed to arrive at Midland?

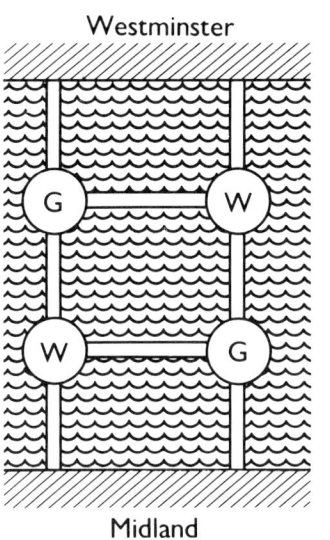

8a BELT UP

The picture shows five double pulleys driven by belts from the left-hand one.
This turns round five times every second in the direction shown and the belts do not slip.
The radius of the outer pulleys is twice the radius of the inner ones.
Draw a diagram to show which way each of the pulleys turns.

How fast does the right-hand one turn?

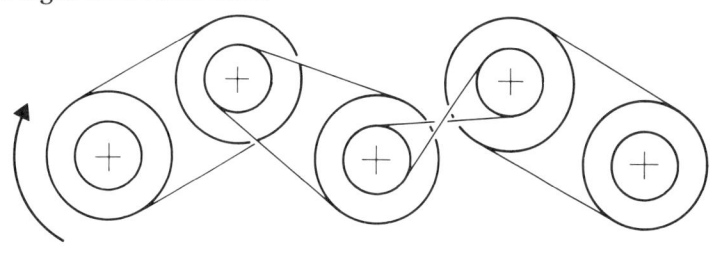

8b LOGIC

The Mathematical Education on Merseyside logo consists of a cube in space with a planet orbiting it.
Each face of the cube has either the letter M or the letter E on it, placed in such a way that whenever three faces are in view, two M's and an E are visible.

What are the letters on the three far sides of the logo pictured here? Is there any choice?

© OUP 1990. This page may be reproduced for class use within the purchaser's institute

8c BEAST OF BURDEN

A smuggler has six sacks of loot, weighing 7, 11, 19, 23, 37 and 49 pounds.

How should he distribute these between the two panniers of his donkey, without opening any of the bags, so that the load is as evenly distributed as possible?

8d SECOND RATE

In 1986 these were the postage rates:

Weight (not more than)	60 g	100 g	150 g	200 g
First class	17 p	24 p	31 p	38 p
Second class	12 p	18 p	22 p	28 p

I had several packages to post, none weighing over 200 g.
If I had sent them first class, the total bill would have been exactly one pound.

What possible amounts might I have paid to send them all second class?

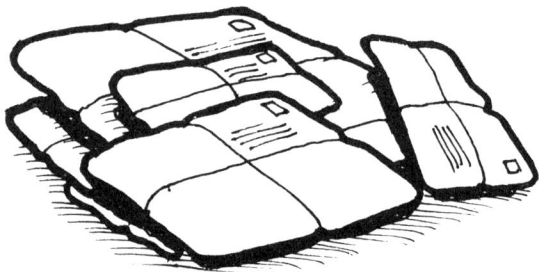

8e PLAN FOR REDUNDANCY

A bankrupt town council made its town planner redundant and then asked him to design, in his new leisure, a one-way street system to ease their traffic problem.
He offered them this map. The arrows indicate the direction of the traffic.

Can you get from A to every street in the town?
Can you leave the town from every street?

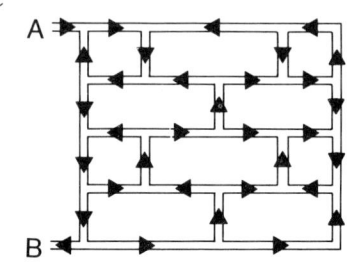

9a THE RIGHT TIMES

How many times in the course of 24 hours are the hands of a clock at right angles to each other?

9b SUPER SHELL

A gutter consists of three equal sections. Two snails have a race along it.
Steven Snail goes at constant speed for all the course.
Sebastian Snail does the first section at twice Steven's speed, the second at the same speed as Steven, and the last section at half the speed of Steven.

Who wins, and by how far?

9c ANNELID vs GASTROPOD

Fresh from his battle with Sebastian Snail, speedy Steve Snail is challenged by an athletic worm to seven laps round an upturned bucket.
Steve goes twice as fast as the worm.

If they start off together, how many times are they together altogether in the course of the course?

9d MR COMPOST

Mr Compost goes to a Garden Centre to buy plants for his garden. Rhododendron bushes cost £5, roses £1 and bedding plants 5p each. He buys at least one of each of these varieties, 100 plants in all.

If he spends exactly £100 how many of each has he bought?

9e TEAM WORK

A party of seven youngsters is entering an orienteering competition. According to the rules no team can have fewer than two or more than three members.
In how many different ways could the seven be enrolled?

10a INSURANCE ANGLE

A disc has all the capital letters of the alphabet and all ten digits evenly spaced round it in order. It can be rotated in either direction and is used to print the symbols on a tape. One rotates the disc until the required symbol is opposite the arrow and then presses. The tape moves on automatically. The digit 0 is different from the letter O.

What is the smallest total angle through which the disc must be turned to print ROYAL, with R opposite the arrow to begin with?

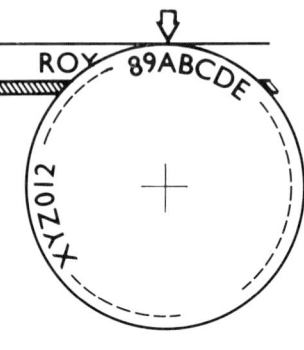

10b GRANNIE'S SECRET

In 1988, my Grannie was quite a bit older than Grandpa. In fact the difference between the *squares* of their ages (amazingly!) was exactly 1988.

How old were they?

10c BEST FRIEND

Some of the five people Alex, Ben, Chris, Dan and Emma are friends with each other. Each pair of friends has just one friend in common. For example, Chris and Dan are friends and the only friend they have in common is Ben. Emma and Chris are friends and have Alex as joint friend but not Ben or Dan.

Is any of the five a friend of all the other four?

10d SPACE INVADERS

As you perhaps know, the male inhabitants of the planet Urno have five antennae while the females have seven.
Recently the famous astronomer Sir Patrick Lesse saw an Urnian flying teacup through his telescope and he counted forty-six antennae altogether.

Assuming that all the antennae were visible and correctly counted, how many of each sex of Urnians were there in the flying teacup?

The following week there was an attempted Urnian invasion when Sir Patrick counted one hundred and forty antennae in all.
In how many different ways could this number have been made up?

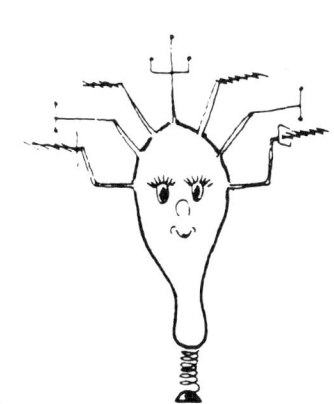

10e POSTAL ORDER

The postmaster of the town of Frankfurter wants to renumber the five postal districts.
At present (see map) if you add up the differences between numbers of districts next to each other

(that is, $(5-1) + (3-2) + (4-2) +$ and so on)

you get 16.

Check this answer, and then, leaving number 1 where it is, rearrange the numbers of the other four districts so that the sum you get in the same way as before is as small as possible.

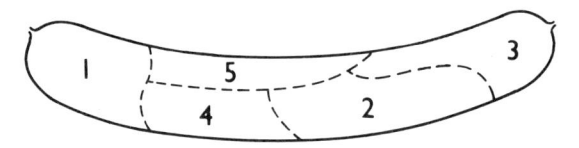

1a MAGIC IT!

Fill in, if you can, the rest of this 'Magic Square' with whole numbers so that the numbers in each row add up to the same total as the numbers in each column and to the same as the numbers in each of the two diagonals.

5		9
	3	7

1b PRESENTS A PROBLEM

I sent two Valentine parcels this year: they were both cubes of side 10 cm.
Without disclosing their contents I shall reveal that I pasted a ribbon round one parcel, starting it off as shown by the dotted lines, and continuing to wrap it round until it just closed up. How many faces did it touch?
How long was it?

On the other parcel, to avoid an embarrassing mix-up, I slanted the ribbon, starting it off as shown, and angling it round the edges so that it lay flat on each face until it just closed up.
How many faces did it touch?
How long was it?

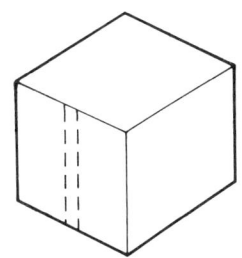

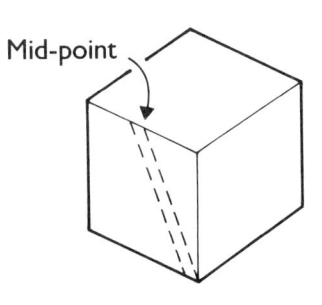

Mid-point

1c IT'S A KNOCKOUT

In arranging a knock-out chess competition the secretary had drawn the first round consisting of a number of matches and a number of byes, so that there would be 32 competitors in the next round.
He then found an envelope containing four entries which he had overlooked. So he had to make the draw again and this time he got as many matches in the first round as he had byes at the first attempt.

What was the total number of entries to the competition?

1d BUSY BEES

A colony of bees is making a honeycomb consisting of hexagonal cells, as in the picture.
They start with the centre cell. The next day they add the six cells round the centre cell, and on the third day they add the remaining ring of cells in the picture.
Every day they add a new ring of cells right round the honeycomb.

How many cells will there be at the end of the sixth day?
On which day will the number of cells pass the 1000 mark?

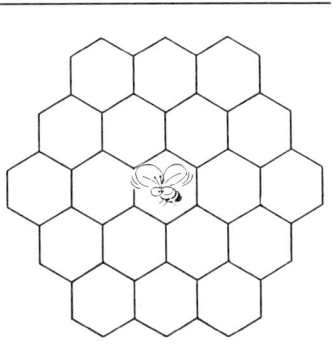

© OUP 1990. This page may be reproduced for class use within the purchaser's institute

1e REVOLUTIONARY

This is part of a bottling machine. Each of the two parts, the crank with the peg attached to it and the Geneva wheel, are mounted on axles.

Describe the behaviour of the Geneva wheel when the crank is turned clockwise at a steady rate.

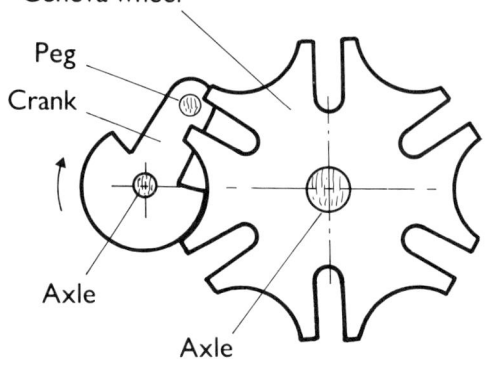

2a CHIMPS ARE CHAMPS

The Animal Hockey League has four teams: the Chimps, Wombats, Zebras and Lions.

Each team plays the other three and the league table is given below, where a win counts 2 points, a draw 1 point, and a defeat no points.

Unfortunately, all the league secretary (an Elephant) can remember is that the Zebras drew 1–1 against the Lions.

Your job is to work out the scores in all the six games played.

	Games played	Games won	Games drawn	Games lost	Goals for	Goals against	Points
Chimps	3	2	1	0	5	1	5
Wombats	3	0	3	0	0	0	3
Zebras	3	0	2	1	2	3	2
Lions	3	0	2	1	1	4	2

2b INSECTICIDE

An insect and two bugs are confined to the six equal arms of the network in space shown in the diagram (technically known as a regular tetrahedral framework!).
All three can move along the arms as they please and can always see each other.
The insect can go twice as fast as one of the bugs but the other bug, being elderly, can only move very slowly.
The bugs try to catch the insect.
Can they do this if they start from where they are shown in the picture?

2c COGGLY

This is the innards of a weird robot animal. A and B operate the feet and C, D and E other parts. The cogs are all on fixed axles.
If A is raised by one centimetre, which way and by how much does B move?
If E moves twenty degrees in the clockwise direction, in which direction do C and D move and by how much?

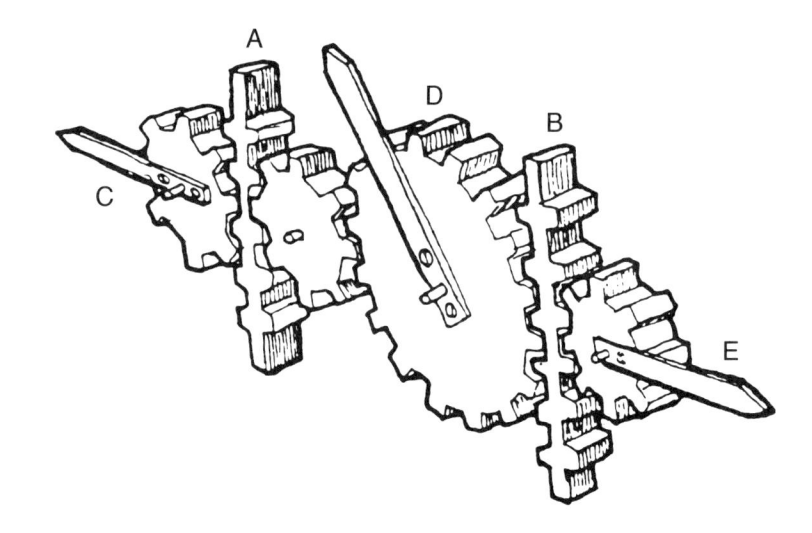

2d TWICE TWO

$1 \cdot \square\square \times 1 \cdot \square\square \times 1 \cdot \square\square = 2$

One solution to the above equation is $1 \cdot 00 \times 1 \cdot 25 \times 1 \cdot 60 = 2$.
Can you find a different solution? (Not just changing the order of multiplication.) Each number is allowed only *two* decimal places.

2e FINAL CHALLENGE

In the CHALLENGE grid below, when moving from one letter to the next you must move towards the right, diagonally up or down along the lines. One letter L is underlined once.

How many ways are there to get from C to this L?
How many ways from C to the L underlined twice?
How many ways from C to the final E? (Each way spells CHALLENGE.)

3a PLOT PLANTS

I have a square garden, with my house in the middle, and I have divided the garden into eight square plots of land, as shown in the diagram.

I want to plant twenty trees, with at least one tree and no more than four trees in any one plot.

Also, I want there to be seven trees in each of the four straight lines of three plots.

The diagrams show two ways of doing this, but I count these as the same solution since they use the same set of numbers, 1, 2 and 4.

How many different solutions can you find?

3b SQUARE ROUTES

A rat is trained to run through the maze shown, entering by one of the two doors and leaving by the other and visiting each of the sixteen compartments once and once only on the way.

We have illustrated one way he could have gone.
Find all his other possible routes through.

How many ways through are there if the upper door is into the top left-hand compartment and not as shown?

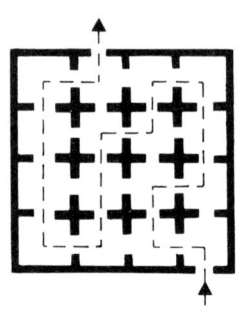

3c DIG THIS

This treasure map shows part of a remote Pacific island.
On the back it says: 'The treasure is buried at the same distance from the coconut tree and the banana tree. The treasure is also twice as far from the mango tree as it is from the cliff edge.'

Make an accurate copy of the map, marking the centres of the trees and the cliff edge, and put a cross on the exact spot where the treasure is buried.

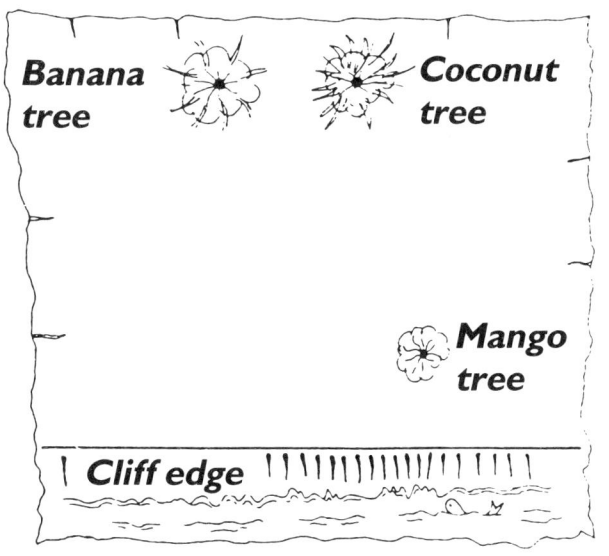

3d COUNTER FEAT

Lisa is a whizz at programming her computer, Ultravox, which can talk, non-stop.
Ultravox can say each of the figures 'nought', 'one', 'two', up to 'nine', and says a number after nine by saying the figures in order.
So for example 27 becomes 'two seven' and 710 becomes 'seven one nought'.
The computer takes half a second to say each figure and pauses for half a second after saying each complete number.
Lisa programs Ultravox to count from 1 to 1,000,000.

How many seconds will Ultravox take?
To the nearest minute, how many minutes?
How many hours?
And lastly, to the nearest day, how many days?

3e DRINK PROBLEM

Our coffee jug holds four times as much as our milk jug.
We all have the same size cup but we like different amounts of milk in our coffee. Jane likes half milk and half coffee; Jean, Joan and June each like one quarter milk, and I like black coffee.
I fill up our five cups the way we each like, and just empty one of the jugs.
How much liquid is left in the other?

4a DAVY JONES'S LOCKER

Davy Jones has forgotten the number of his locker.
The combination is a five-digit number, each digit being one of the numbers 0, 1, 2, 3, 4, 5.
All he can remember about the correct number is

- the first three digits add up to 4;
- the fifth digit is greater than the fourth.

Only knowing this information, how many combinations might be correct if repetitions of digits are not allowed?
How many if repetitions of digits are allowed?

4b RAFFLE BAFFLER

The Refuge for Battered Fish sells 2000 raffle tickets in books of five, numbered 1 to 5, 6 to 10, and so on, up to 1996 to 2000.
The winning ticket is the middle one in a book.
When you add up the five ticket numbers in that book, the answer has each of the ten numbers 1, 2, 3, 4, 5, 6, 7, 8, 9 and 10 as a factor.
Which is the winning ticket?

4c ROOMS WITH A VIEW

An architect is asked to design a bungalow with five rectangular rooms each with a window.
There has to be a door from A to each of B, C, D; from B to A and C; from C to B, A and D; from D to A, C and E; from E to D.
Draw the plan of such a bungalow.

4d ADVERSE CONDITIONS

The map shows available railway track from town A to town B.
Due to adverse weather conditions the number of trains per hour on different parts of the network was limited one day to the numbers shown.

Under these conditions what is the greatest number of trains that the railway company could have sent all the way from A to B per hour?

Draw the diagram again and put on each section of track the actual number of trains which run along it, together with their direction.

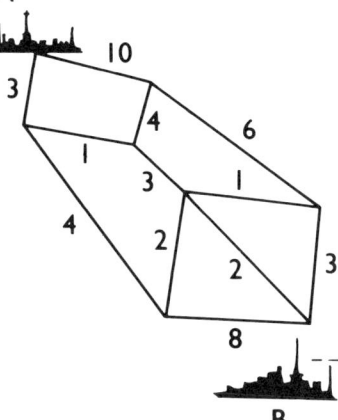

4e ESCALATION

There are 54 steps visible at any one time on one of the Merseyrail escalators.
Peter, who runs twice as fast as Ann walks, manages to go up 36 steps before reaching the top.

How many steps has Ann climbed before she gets to the top?

5a PLOTTING AND PLANNING

A chemical firm want to test how good their latest four weedkillers are.
They have a field covered in weeds but of course the weeds are growing in different places and with different amounts of water, light etc.
To make the test spraying fair the field is divided into sixteen plots and one of the weedkillers, A, B, C or D applied to each, as seen in the incomplete diagram.

A	B	C	D
B			
C			
D			

Can you find all the ways of completing the diagram so that all four plots going across or down have different treatments?

5b FOUR SQUARE

Albert doubled Brenda's money (that is, gave Brenda as much money as she already had), then Brenda doubled Chris's money, then Chris doubled Dan's money and finally Dan doubled Albert's money. Then they all had £16.

How much did each start with?

5c SUM HOW

In the picture, ten cards numbered 0 to 9 have been arranged correctly to form an addition sum.
There are other arrangements of the ten cards where two three-figure numbers add to give a four-figure number.

Find as many of these as you can.

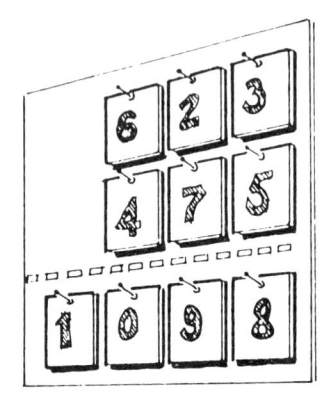

5d CARTOGRAPHY

An island has just five small towns on it.
Coldharbour is at the North end, and Eastward Ho is on the Eastern side, as you would expect.
Aberavon, Burnmouth and Downside also lie on the coast.
There are just two roads. One goes all the way round the coast, passing through each of the towns, while the other goes across the island, from one of the towns to another one.
The mileage table shows the shortest distances by road between the five towns.

Make a road map of the island.

	A	B	C	D
B	4			
C	7	11		
D	2	3	9	
E	6	7	10	4

40 © OUP 1990. This page may be reproduced for class use within the purchaser's institute

5e ON THE CARDS

Joe Ninety was looking very pleased with himself, and not surprisingly, for it was his ninetieth birthday.

'I've just realized,' he said, 'that if you multiply together the ages of my three great-grandchildren, you get exactly 90. They're all under 15, too.'

I asked Joe how old his great-grandchildren were, and he replied, with a wink, 'Well, if you add their ages instead of multiplying them, you get the number of birthday cards on the mantelpiece.'

I counted the cards, thought for a moment, and still couldn't work out their ages.

How many birthday cards were there on the mantelpiece?

6a JOB OPPORTUNITIES

A foreman is responsible for allocating work to eight operators, whom we shall call A, B, C, D, E, F, G and H.
Five have to work machines numbered 1, 2, 3, 4 and 5, one operator per machine.

The foreman knows that the value of goods produced per hour by each operator on each machine is as is shown in the following table:

	1	2	3	4	5
A	2	5	7	4	4
B	8	8	8	6	5
C	9	5	8	3	3
D	2	5	2	8	6
E	4	5	8	7	3
F	7	2	2	5	2
G	9	8	9	8	7
H	3	8	7	4	6

For example, operator D on machine 2 produces £5 worth of goods per hour.

There are several ways the foreman can allocate the operators to the machines to ensure that £40 of goods are produced per hour. What are these ways?

6b CLOSE ENCOUNTERS

A town has 6000 inhabitants and at 8 am someone comes to the town with the news that green men from Sirius have landed five miles away.
Immediately he arrives he tells three people the news.
They hurry away and at 8.10 am each of them tells three other people in the town. At 8.20 am each person who heard the news at 8.10 am tells it to three more people. This continues so that, every ten minutes, more people hear the news.
Assuming that no-one tells or hears the news twice, by what time will at least half the population of the town have heard the news? How many will know the news then?

6c ACROSS THE BOARD

The diagram shows one way of going from top left to bottom right of a 4 × 4 board, each move being one square → or ↓ or ↘.

How many ways are there altogether?

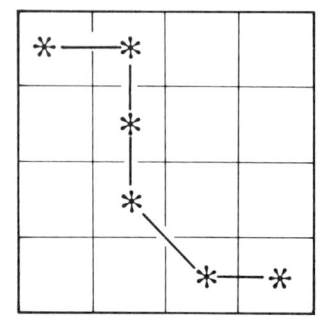

6d WRAP UP

Kathy has bought a thin book, 6 inches by 8 inches, as a present for her sister, and is puzzled as to which of three sheets of left-over Christmas paper she should use to wrap it up completely.
One of these is 9 inches by 9 inches, one 11 inches by 11 inches and the third 13 inches by 13 inches.

Which is the smallest sheet she need use?
Indicate by a diagram how the wrapping should be done.

6e WIND BAND

Three boys, David, Gareth and Leslie, live in the same street.
Of the three one is a keen angler, another swims for his school, while the third belongs to the local Judo club.
Each plays an instrument in the school wind band, one the flute, one the clarinet, and the third the trombone. Leslie lives halfway between the angler and the trombone player.
David and the angler are cousins. Gareth and the clarinet player support different football teams.

What instrument does each of the boys play?

7a FAIR PLAY

Three youngsters were playing darts at the fair on this rather unusual board.

Each had six throws and every dart hit the target, but the bull's eye was hit only once.

Dave scored 120, Karen 110 and Steve 100.

What were the six hits that each made?

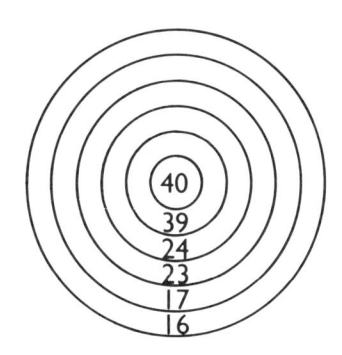

7b SEXTUPLETS

Twin girls may be identical or non-identical, while with triplet girls there are three possibilities, all three identical, two identical and one not, or all three non-identical.

With sextuplet girls how many possibilities are there?

7c METRIC RULES

I want to be able to draw lines of lengths exactly one centimetre, two centimetres, or any other whole number of centimetres up to twelve centimetres, each line to be drawn with the ruler in a fixed position.

I have a piece of wood exactly twelve centimetres long.

What is the smallest number of marks I need to put on the wood so that I can do this?

12 cm

7d HIC!

A barrel contains 24 pints of beer which are to be shared equally by three people.

Unfortunately there are only three containers available, one holding 5 pints, one 11 pints, and one 13 pints.

If one person is going to take his share home in the barrel how should the containers be used to give each man his share?

(It is not possible to pour beer back into the barrel!)

7e ACID TEST

A cube of metal is suspended by a corner and lowered into acid until exactly half the volume is submerged.
The metal below the surface of the acid dissolves completely.

What is the shape of the new bottom face of the block of metal?

8a MARK THIS

Competitors in a maths competition can score 0, 1, 2 or 3 marks on each of the six questions.
There is only one way of scoring 18, and there are six ways of scoring 17.

How many ways are there of scoring 16?

8b BALL POINTS

A number of leather squares and triangles are sewn together to form a ball.
The edges of the squares and triangles are all of the same length and at each corner three squares and one triangle meet.

How many squares and how many triangles are required altogether and how many such meeting points are there?

8c ANATHEMATICS

Nine nutters sit down to a working lunch.
All are from mathematical pressure groups, three from the Abolish Algebra Action Group, three from Stamp Out Geometry, and three from Banish All Arithmetic.

There are, going clockwise round the table, various possible pairs of neighbours, such as (SOG)(AAAG) or (BAA)(BAA) or (AAAG)(SOG). Write down all *nine* such possible pairs.

The Chairnutters of the three pressure groups are already seated as shown, and they insist that, reading clockwise round the table, all these nine pairs of neighbours should occur.
How can the other six seats be allocated to the pressure groups?
Is there more than one solution?

8d CUBE ROUTES

The picture shows a 2 × 2 × 2 cube hung from one of its corners.
It also shows one way of going steadily downwards from the top to the bottom, keeping to lines or edges all the way.

How many such routes are there in all?

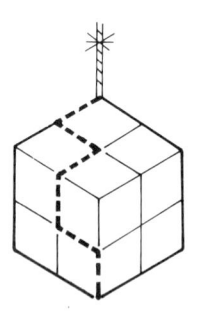

8e THE LAST ONE

In a normal set of 28 dominoes the double six is laid down.
If you lay the dominoes down in the usual way, but working in one direction only, until they are all used or until you get stuck, what is the number at the end of the last domino?
Can you say why?

John is playing in both directions from the double six and finds that he can use all of his dominoes.
His sister Jane then says that she hid one before he started.
Can John always say immediately which one it is?

46 © OUP 1990. This page may be reproduced for class use within the purchaser's institute

1 CHAIN REACTION

Think of any three-figure number, for example 187.

Put the figures in descending order	871	963	954	954
Reverse the digits	178	369	459	
Subtract	693	594	495	

Each time you subtract you use the answer as the new starting point.

In the example above the numbers at the top of the third and fourth columns are the same.

By starting with other three-figure numbers you can increase the number of steps before the chain ends.

Write down the longest chain you can find.
You could also investigate four-figure numbers.

2 DOWNHILL ALL THE WAY

The diagram shows a goods siding which slopes gently downhill from West (W) to East (E), with buffers at the bottom of the slope on each branch (called North (N) and South (S)).

A goods train stands on the W section, the train consisting of an engine and five waggons, labelled 4, 1, 3, 5, 2 in order.

It is necessary to rearrange them in the order 1, 2, 3, 4, 5. The only 'moves' allowed are like this: the waggons are uncoupled one by one and rolled down the slope either into the N or the S branch. Then the engine picks up first all those in the N branch, then all those in the S branch.

Finally the engine pulls the waggons back into the W section.

For example,

$$41352 \begin{cases} 12 \\ 435 \end{cases}$$

would lead to the order 12435.

Can you find another 'move' to follow this one which will end with the order 12345?

Suppose the starting order was 54321. Show how to change this into 12345 with as few moves as you can.

Start with other orders and change them into 12345 in as few moves as possible.

3 + = ×

Can you find three whole numbers, each between one and ten (inclusive), which give the same answer when you multiply all of them together as when you add all of them together?

Can you find a collection of five whole numbers having the same property? (The five numbers need not all be different.)

Find as many collections of five numbers as you can.

Can you find *all* possibilities?

4 POWER CUTS

Stout wire is available only in certain lengths, which in feet are powers of two, i.e. 2 ft, 4 ft, 8 ft, 16 ft, 32 ft and so on, doubling each time.
The wire can only be cut by machine.

I have a machine which will cut any whole number of *yards* off a piece of this wire. (In case you've forgotten, three feet make a yard!) How can I make pieces of wire whose lengths in feet are all the whole numbers from 1 to 20 inclusive?

Do you think I could make a wire whose length was *any* whole number of feet?

5 SPADEWORK

Nine cards, the One (Ace) to the Nine of Spades, are lying face up on the table between you and me.
We take turns in playing one of these cards at a time on to a central pile, where the card then stays. There is only one rule.
Each card played, after the first one, must have a number which is a *multiple* or a *factor* of the previous one.
For example, if one of us plays the 4, then the other must play the 1, 2 or 8, provided that one of these is still available.
The loser is the first of us unable to play.
  (i) Suppose that you start. Why can you be sure to have beaten me after only three cards have been played?
 (ii) Suppose that I start, with one of the *even* numbered cards. Can you always beat me?

6 CORNERED

The picture shows a rectangle 3 cm by 6 cm divided into one-centimetre squares. As you can see, the diagonal passes through four points (marked with a dot) which are corners of squares. Starting with a rectangle 24 cm by 36 cm, divided into one-centimetre squares, through how many points which are corners of squares does the diagonal pass?
What is the effect on this number of changing **one** of the dimensions of the rectangle by 1 cm?

What happens for other sizes of rectangle?
(And what happens for a rectangular solid block made up of one-centimetre *cubes*?)

7 GRINDING AWAY

Two interlocking cog wheels have 24 and 15 teeth as in the picture. There is a small stone stuck between two of the teeth on the larger wheel.
With how many different teeth of the smaller wheel will this eventually come into contact when the wheels are turning?

If the number of teeth on one of the cog wheels were one different from the number given, could the stone eventually come into contact with ALL the teeth of the other wheel?

See what happens with other numbers of cogs on the two wheels.

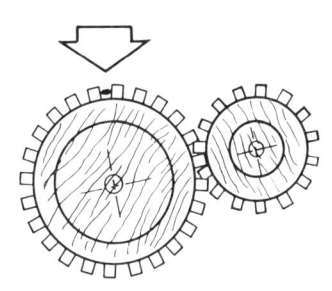

8 COUNTDOWN

There are three objects – a knife, a fork and a spoon – on the table. Three children, Alison, Bill and Chris, each pick up one of these, not letting you see who chooses which.
There is also a pile of 18 counters on the table.
You give 1 to Alison, 2 to Bill and 3 to Chris. 'Now', you say, 'while my back is turned, I want the person who has the knife to take the same number of counters as I have just given him or her. Also the person who has the fork is to take twice as many as I have just given and the one who has the spoon four times as many.'

Make a chart to show all the possible ways in which the three objects could have been picked up by the three children.
For each way work out how many counters are left at the end.

Can you tell, just by looking at the number of counters left, which child has which object?

Investigate what happens when Alison, Bill and Chris are given other numbers of counters to begin with. You may need to increase the pile of 18 to a higher number as well.

© OUP 1990. This page may be reproduced for class use within the purchaser's institute

9 ARC LIGHT

There was a young glowworm called Glim,
Who went for a ride on the rim
    Of a wheel that went round
    As it rolled on the ground.
Please draw me the arc traced by him!

(And what if Glim rode, rather more safely, on some other part of the wheel?)

10 MOWER TIME

A garden contains two identical 10 ft × 15 ft rectangular lawns. Chris and Alex have a mowing race.
Each has a mower which cuts a 1 ft strip of grass but they use quite different methods. Chris mows back and forth in strips while Alex chooses a spiral pattern (see diagrams).
The 180° turns take 5 seconds and the 90° turns take 2 seconds. (Neither Chris nor Alex is worried about the tiny areas which remain uncut when they make a turn!)
On the assumption that Chris and Alex start at the same time and walk at the same speed, who finishes first?

What must be the time taken for 180° turns if they are to finish at exactly the same time?

Do the dimensions of the two identical rectangular lawns make any difference to these answers?

What if Chris and Alex start by going along the *short* side of the rectangle?

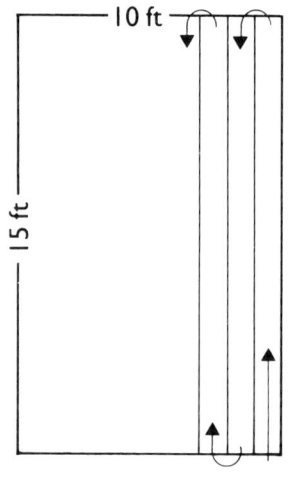

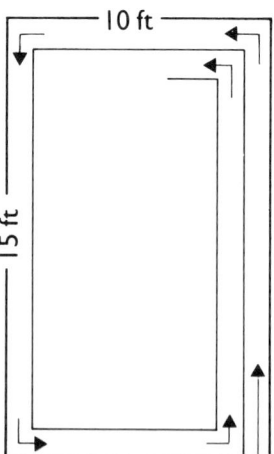

11 SLIPPED DISC

A gramophone record has a spiral groove which winds anticlockwise from the edge to the label in the centre.
The record is cut straight across, along a diameter, and, keeping the record flat, one half is moved by the width of the groove.
What happens to the spiral?
What happens if the displacement is by twice the width of the groove? (Experiment by drawing a diagram rather than by cutting an actual record in half!)

What about three or more groove widths?

12 CIRCLE LINE

On a circular railway round which trains go in either direction there are a main station and two suburban stations.
The suburban stations are sited in such a way that in some sense or other each is twice as far round the track from the main station as the other one is.

Draw a map of the railway.
(This is an easy introduction to the next question.)

13 NEW CIRCLE LINE

On a circular railway round which trains go in either direction there are a main station M and *three* suburban stations A, B and C.
Suppose you get on at M and off at A.
Then there are lots of different distances you could cover, depending on which way round you went, and on how many times you went round before getting off.
Now the stations are sited so that no matter how far you travel in going from M to *each one* of A, B or C you could travel exactly twice as far in the same direction to arrive at one of the other two.

What are the possible sites for the stations?

(Apart from changing around the letters A, B, C there are two essentially different solutions. Of course, the same question can be asked about M and *four* suburban stations A, B, C and D!)

14 LET'S FACE IT

A supply of equilateral (equal-sided) coloured triangles of the right size is available for sticking, four at a time, on to a regular tetrahedral framework, to make a regular tetrahedron (or triangular pyramid).
Suppose first that the triangles are all either red or blue (colours of Liverpool and Everton!).
Then five different tetrahedra can be made, one all red, one with three red sides and one blue side, one with two red sides and two blue sides, one with one red side and three blue sides and one all blue.

How many different tetrahedra can be made with these triangles if *three* different colours are available, say red, blue and green?
How many can be made if *four* different colours are available, say red, blue, green and yellow?

15 VALHALLA

This is the board for a game for two players, Val and Hal. The pieces are dominoes each of which covers exactly two squares of the board.

Val places her dominoes vertically

and Hal places his horizontally.

Each plays alternately and either may play first.
The first player unable to play is the loser. Which player should win and what moves ensure victory?

You can also start with different boards, but keep the same rules about horizontal and vertical dominoes.

16 DAMP COURSE

A sadistic schoolmaster devises the following punishment to encourage his boys to spend more time on geometry.
A victim is placed at the centre of a circle above the edge of which three pails of cold water are suspended.
These are equally spaced round the circle, and can be moved round it in either direction by a mechanism designed and controlled by the master in such a way that at all times they remain at the same distance from each other.
The pails can travel twice as fast as a boy can run and any pail automatically empties itself over a boy if he passes underneath.

Can the victim escape from the circle without getting a wetting?

17 NIGHT AT THE ROUND TABLE

In a nightmare you find yourself having to sit at a large round table at which three people you don't care for too much are already seated.
Where should you place your chair so that, when you add up the shortest distances round the edge of the table from yourself to each of the three nasties, the answer that you get is as large as possible?

18 FEARSOME FOURSOME

Another nightmare!
This time there are *four* nasties round the table, and again you have to sit so that the sum of the shortest distances from yourself to the nasties round the edge of the table is as large as possible.
Whereabouts should you go this time?

19 SPACE MEN

By sticking together five 1 cm cubes face to face one can form one **linear man**

or any one of eleven **plane men**, such as

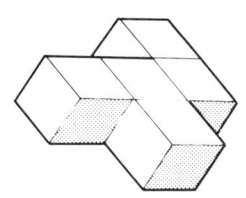

or

A linear man or a plane man can always lie down in such a way that all of his five cubes touch the ground.

But, still using only five cubes joined face to face, there are over a dozen **space men**, who cannot lie flat on the ground, such as

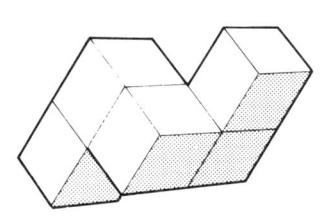

and

A **space capsule** is a 2 cm × 2 cm × 2 cm cubical box.

Would any of the space men fit into such a capsule and, if so, which?

20 GEMINI

Castor and Pollux are space twins.
Though Pollux is distinct from Castor, he is of course his mirror image.
On the other hand, neither two-headed Sirius nor Pluto is distinguishable from his mirror image.
How many space men are there altogether, and amongst them how many pairs of space twins are there?

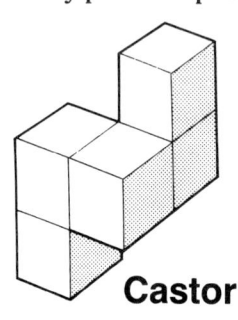

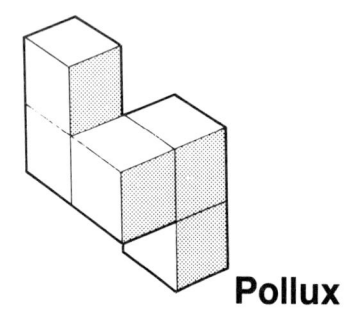

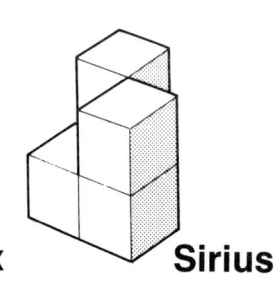

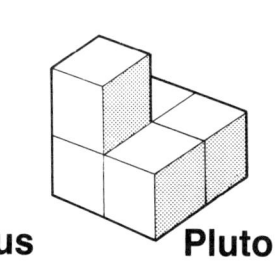

Castor   **Pollux**   **Sirius**   **Pluto**

1a I'S DOWN

There are many solutions, and one is shown in the diagram on the right.

7	8	5	5	5
7	8	6	6	6
7	8	■	3	4
1	1	1	3	4
2	2	2	3	4

1b ICE ACROSS

The volume of icing is $1 \times 30 \times 30 = 900$ cubic centimetres.
The volume of icing needed for one rectangular cake is
$(1/2) \times 12 \times 20 = 120$ cubic centimetres.
So Ken can ice 900/120 or 7 whole cakes, with a bit of icing left over (enough for half a cake, but who wants a half-iced cake?).

1c WHOLESUM

There are lots of triples of numbers adding up to 10 but very few multiplying up to 30, in fact only 1, 2, 15; 1, 3, 10; 1, 5, 6; and 2, 3, 5.
Now $2 + 3 + 5 = 10$.
So the numbers are 2, 3 and 5.

1d CORRECT!

Two of the three numbers 123, 297, 330 are correct.
So the only candidates for the correct sum are
$33 + 297 = 330$, $123 + 297 = 420$ and $123 + 207 = 330$.
Only the last one fits the problem.

1e WHERE ALFRED FAILED

The important part of this question is the loop, checking, perhaps several times, whether the cake is cooked.
A correct solution is

1. Switch on the oven.
2. Wait 30 minutes.
3. Put the cake in the oven.
4. Wait 20 minutes.
5. Is the cake cooked?
6. If yes, proceed to step 9; if no, proceed to step 7.
7. Wait 5 minutes.
8. Return to step 5.
9. Take cake out of oven.
10. Switch off the oven.

There were several acceptable variants.
For example, 9 and 10 in our order can be interchanged.
In the competition, some people with gas ovens at home quite properly complained that 30 minutes was needlessly long for the oven to heat up.
What we forgot to tell was what heat to set the oven at!

2a A POWERFUL START

$2^{11} - 2^6 = 2048 - 64 = 1984$.
So $n = 11, m = 6$.

2b L-ISH

There are many solutions, one of which is shown on the right.
Note that it is not, in fact, necessary to turn any of the L's over.

6	6	3	3	3
5	6	3	1	1
5	6	2	2	1
5	5	4	2	1
4	4	4	2	

2c JOINERY

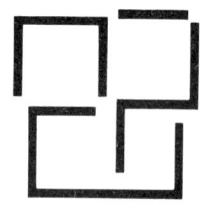

2d AGE-OLD PROBLEM

The combined age of four people increases by 4 each year.
If it is 100 in ten years' time, it will be 80 in five years' time.

2e APPROPRIATE STEPS

Three steps are needed.
Let the feet of the ladder be at A and B and let ABC be an equilateral triangle.
Then
1. rotate ladder about foot A so that B moves to C;
2. rotate about C so that A moves to B;
3. rotate about B so that C moves to A.

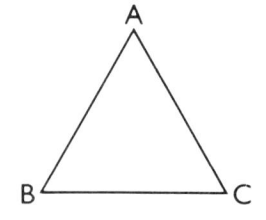

3a INITIAL CHALLENGE

(As you might guess, this problem was set in 1981!)

3b 4L = L

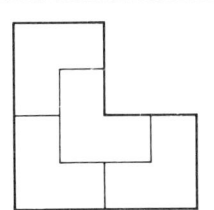

3c DRAWN AND QUARTERED

The only way to make the sloping line is as shown.
To make the rest, shaded in the diagram, one piece must be turned over.

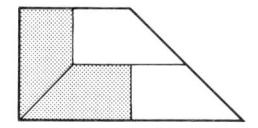

3d FOOD FOR THOUGHT

Since chips cost 45p more than mash and since egg and chips cost 150p it follows that *egg* and *mash* ought to *cost 105p* (though it probably wouldn't in real life!).
It isn't possible, from what you are given, to work out the cost of the separate ingredients.

3e MIXED UP

The first bottle contains Cyanide, and Arsenic, the second Cyanide, and the third Arsenic.

4a FIT THE FIRST

Only three pieces will fit, though it can be done in many ways, for example:

4b FIT THE SECOND

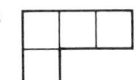

The shape is   It fits like this:

4c GENESIS

Trial and error is good here, guided by factorizing Eve's answers.
Thus $16 = 4 \times 4 = 8 \times 2 = 16 \times 1$ but only $8 + 2 = 10$ so the numbers are 8 and 2.
Similarly they are 8 and 7 in the second case and 21 and 10 in the third case.

If Adam's answer is a and Eve's is e, then the numbers are the two solutions x of the quadratic equation $x^2 - ax + e = 0$, but in order that both values for x are whole numbers we need $a^2 - 4e$ to be a perfect square of the same parity (evenness or oddness) as a.

4d CROSS NUMBER PUZZLE

1 across must end in 0 or 5
2 down divisible by 13 rules out 0 and can only be 52
3 across must be 42
1 down could be 24 or 84, but since the four figures are *different* (many forget this!) it must be 84.

1 8	2 5
3 4	2

4e LA PETITE LOCOMOTIVE

If the rear wheels of the engine turn anticlockwise then the front wheels turn clockwise, because of the way they are connected.
(Needless to say in the competition this question produced a great variety of answers, some relating to the lack of pistons or track, or to the age of the engine or its disputed nationality. These were not regarded as adequate answers.)

5a STARTERS

(i) Call the numbers $n - 1, n$ and $n + 1$. Then adding them gives $3n = 42$, so $n = 14$ and the numbers are 13, 14 and 15.

(ii) Suppose it is now m minutes before 12.
Then $\frac{3}{4}$ of an hour ago it was $60 - (m + 45) = 15 - m$ minutes past 11.
Thus $15 - m = m$ so $m = 7\frac{1}{2}$.

5b TANGRAM

This really is a matter of experimenting.
Solutions:

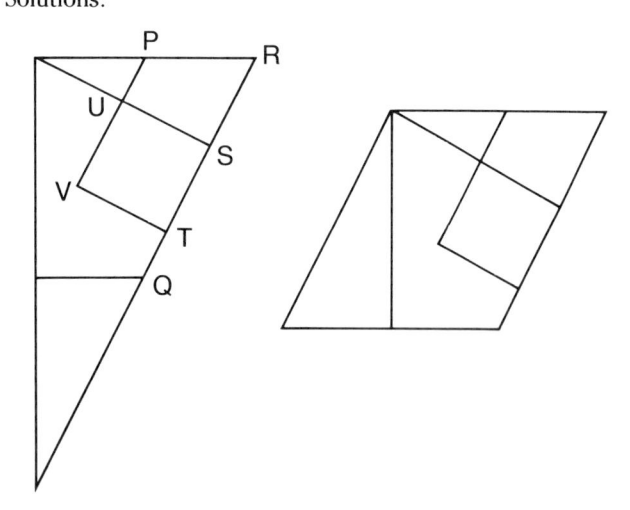

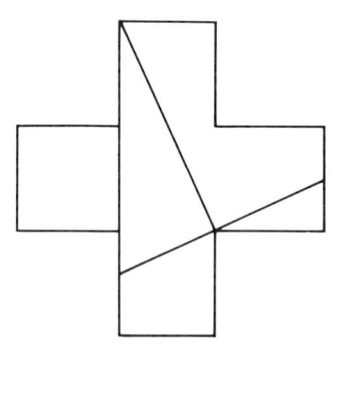

The points P, Q are the mid-points of sides of the big square, and the central piece *is* a square.
It follows that RS = ST = 2TQ = 2PU = UV (if the length PR is 1 then these are all $2/\sqrt{5}$).
From these facts it follows that the Greek cross really *is* a Greek cross!

5c ODD ARRANGEMENTS

There are many solutions.
Here is one for each number:

$5 = 3 + 7 - (5 \times 1)$
$6 = 1 + 3 + 7 - 5$
$7 = 7 \times (5 - 3 - 1)$
$8 = 5 + 7 - 1 - 3$
$9 = 5 + 7 - (1 \times 3)$
$10 = 1 + 5 + 7 - 3$

5d DOWN ON THE FARM

A duck and a goose together cost £9 + £11 = £20.
Moreover $10\,000 = 500 \times 20$.
So there are 500 pairs of birds, 1000 birds in all.

5e STANDING ORDERS

The simple answer is that Fred was waiting patiently for Hilda elsewhere.
A better answer is that they hadn't agreed beforehand which one should stay
in one place if they did get separated.

1a LICK THIS!

The stamps were in horizontal double rows.

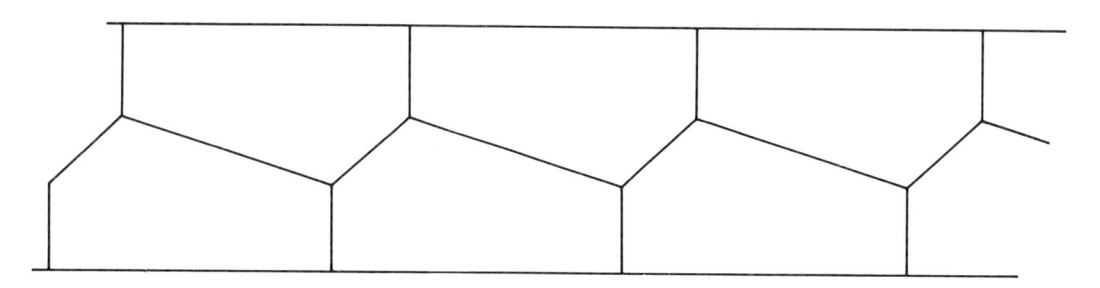

1b GARDEN OF THE YEAR

The only solution that fits the question is
$$1987 = 27^2 + 27^2 + 23^2.$$

One finds this by looking for perfect squares near to $\frac{1}{3}(1987)$.
There are other expressions for 1987 as a sum of three squares, namely
$33^2 + 27^2 + 13^2, 39^2 + 21^2 + 5^2$ and $41^2 + 15^2 + 9^2$, but none of these fits the problem as stated.

1c FERRET THIS OUT!

Call the Ferret's age f.
Then father is $12f$ and I am $3f$.
A time $2f$ ago I was aged f (same as ferret is now); father was $12f - 2f = 10f$.
This is *ten* times my age then.

1d WHEREHOUSE?

Starting at A each mile move towards B increases the number of delivery miles per week by 8 but decreases it by $4 + 7 + 6 = 17$.
From B to C we get $+(8 + 4) - (7 + 6) = -1$, so the number is still going down. After C we get $+(8 + 4 + 7) - 6$, so it goes up.
Hence the best location for the warehouse is at C.

If D requires only 5 deliveries per week then between B and C we get $+(8 + 4) - (7 + 5) = 0$ as the change in the number of delivery miles per week. So in this case *any* of the four mile-marks from B to C is equally good as a possible location for the warehouse.

The total costs, two-way, are £696 and £348, respectively, though this information was not specifically asked for.

1e TIME FOR A SWIM

It is possible to do this by trial and error or by a technique known as 'dynamic programming', where you start at the Pool end of the route and (if you can drag yourself away) work backwards, noting at each junction the shortest time from that junction to the Pool, going North or East at each junction. This produces the diagram shown, and gives the shortest route shown, which takes 18 minutes (there are several routes which take 19 minutes).

It is possible to better this by 1 minute to 17 minutes by going along the route in the right-hand diagram. There is no such simple technique for finding this better route which allows any turn at a junction.

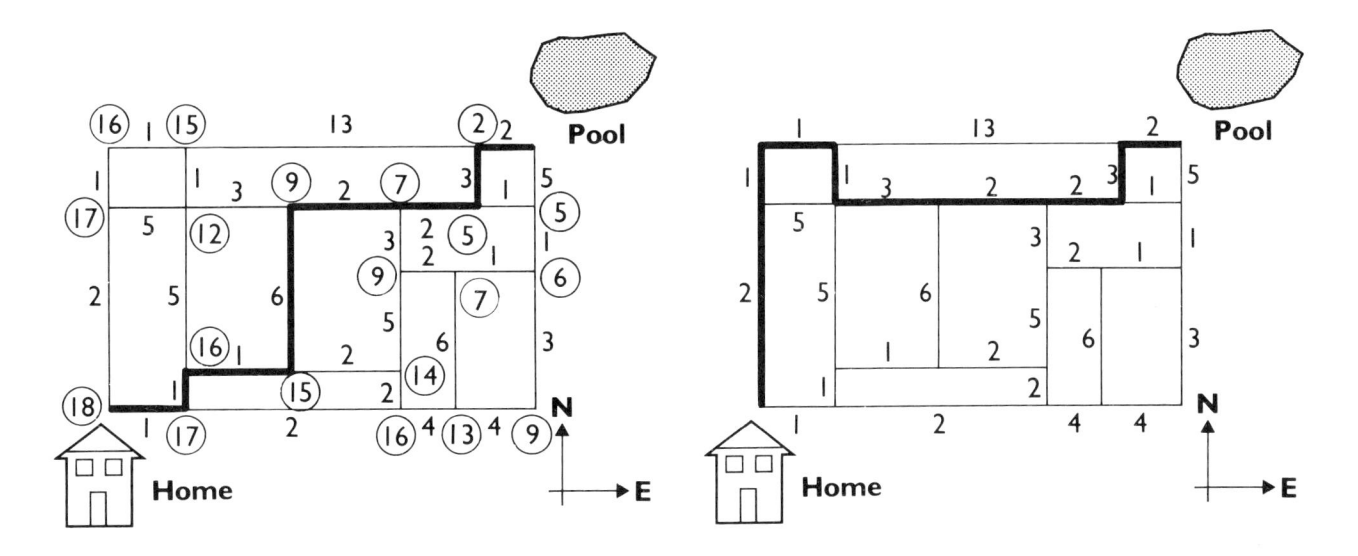

2a ONE GOOD TURN

For every turn of the chain wheel the hub goes round $52/13 = 4$ times, so the distance is $4 \times 2.2 = 8.8$ metres.

2b FIGURE IT OUT

The right-hand sum, of course, only tells you that $A + C = 9$.
From the units column of the left-hand sum, $A + B = 10$, so from the tens column $C + B + 1 = C + 10$ (since $B \neq 0$), which gives $B = 9, A = 1, C = 8$, and the number ABCB is 1989.

2c A SCRATCH CALCULATION

For £12 you get 40 nails + 4 free making 44.
Now 33 nails cost £9.90.
For £10.20 you get 34 + 3 free.
So you can't buy just 35 in a single purchase.

2d PENTAGRAN

The situation is not the same as in TEAM WORK (Part 2, Problem 9e) for here the different permutations of the five old people within the two rows do matter. There are 10 ways they can split into a 3 and a 2, but each 3 can sit in 6 ways, and each 2 in 2 ways, giving 10 times 6 times 2 = 120 ways in all. Or, if we ignore the rows, the first has a choice of 5 seats, after which the second has a choice of 4, then the third a choice of 3, the fourth a choice of 2 and the fifth a 'choice' of 1, giving 5 times 4 times 3 times 2 times 1 = 120 ways in all, as before.

The number 120 is called '5 factorial' and denoted by 5!.

2e PENALTY DECISION

The lowest total is 18, obtained by the following pairings of people and tasks: A-V, B-Y, C-W, D-Z and E-X.
(There are several assignments adding up to 19 penalty points.) The table, and hence the problem, can be simplified if the lowest number in each row is subtracted from all numbers in the row, so getting a table which contains zeros, and then doing the same with the columns to get more zeros (or columns first, then rows).

3a MATCHBOXES

It's probably easiest to work by the number of vertical layers in the block, assuming that the matchboxes are placed with shortest edge vertical.
This number must be a factor of 6, so must be 1, 2, 3, or 6.
In fact suppose the block has p layers.
Let each layer have q boxes in one direction (say that of the middle length edge of a matchbox) and r in the other direction (that of the longest edge of a matchbox). Then $p \times q \times r = 6$ and what we are counting is ways of factorizing 6 where the *order* of the factors is important.
(Notice that we assume the three edges of the matchbox to be of different lengths. Also we could make some different kinds of blocks if say the longest edge happened to be twice the middle length edge, as in the figure. We hoped when setting the question that these exceptional cases would be ignored, and they were!)

The factorizations are

1 layer: $1 \times 1 \times 6$, $1 \times 6 \times 1$, $1 \times 2 \times 3$, $1 \times 3 \times 2$
2 layers: $2 \times 1 \times 3$, $2 \times 3 \times 1$
3 layers: $3 \times 1 \times 2$, $3 \times 2 \times 1$
6 layers: $6 \times 1 \times 1$

Thus $2 \times 1 \times 3$ for example gives this block.

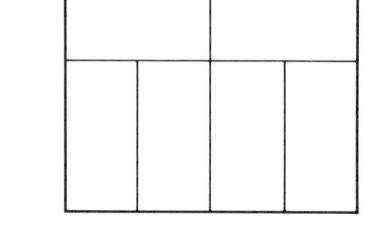

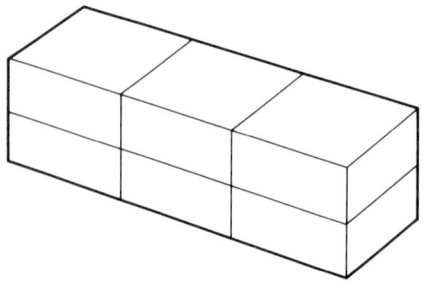

3b SELL OUT

After each sale the number of cakes is $\frac{2}{3}$ of what it was before since one third has been sold. Since there were 8 left after the third sale there must have been 12 after the second, since $8 = \frac{2}{3} \times 12$. There must have been 18 after the first, since $12 = \frac{2}{3} \times 18$, and there must therefore have been 27 *originally*, since $18 = \frac{2}{3} \times 27$.

3c KEY PRODUCTS

When two numbers are added together the answer is called the *sum* and when they are multiplied the answer is called the *product*.
This question concerns products.
You have to find three numbers x, y and z such that

$$yz = 432, zx = 540, xy = 720.$$

You can do this by trying various factorizations of 432 until you find one that fits the other two equations.
Or you can observe that

$$\frac{(zx)(xy)}{yz} = x^2, \text{ so that } x^2 = \frac{(540)(720)}{432} = 900.$$

So $x = 30$, from which it follows that $y = 24$ and $z = 18$.
Either way the key to the code consists of the numbers 30, 24, 18.

3d GLOPPITS

This is a 'linear programming' example, though trial and error works well.
Here is how the algebraic solution works:

If there are x machines of type 1 and y of type 2 then we are told

	$x + y \leq 30$	(1)
Men required:	$x + 2y \leq 50$	(2)
Cost:	$500x + 1500y \leq 40{,}000$, i.e. $x + 3y \leq 80$	(3)
Output:	$30x + 40y$	

so we want to maximize $30x + 40y$ subject to (1), (2) and (3).

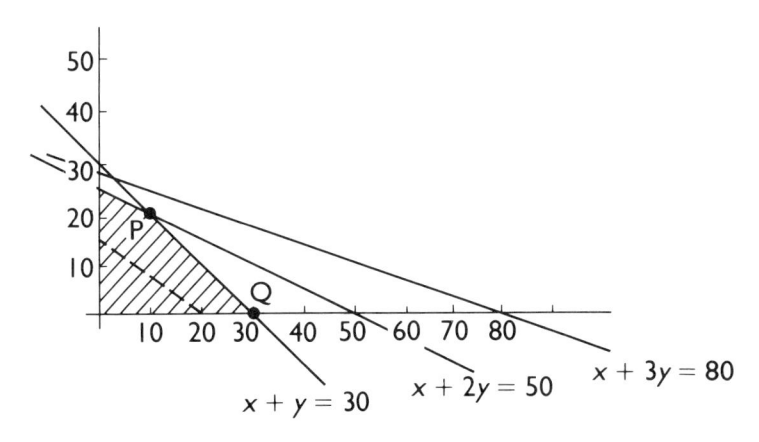

The solution point (x, y) needs to be underneath (or on) all three lines $x + y = 30$, $x + 2y = 50$, $x + 3y = 80$, and also of course $x \geq 0$ and $y \geq 0$.
But notice that the third line $x + 3y = 80$ doesn't give any *extra* condition: this information (total cost $\leq £40{,}000$) is not needed.
Real-life problems are often fraught with redundant information!

Lines $30x + 40y = k$ are all parallel to the dotted line and moving this up as far as possible (to increase k) while still hitting the shaded region it passes through P, which is $x = 10, y = 20$. This is the best solution and it uses the full capacity of the factory (i.e. we get $=$ in (1) and (2)). The cost is
$£(500 \times 10 + 1500 \times 20) = £35{,}000$.

If, say, the output were $40x + 20y$ instead, then the best line $40x + 20y = k$ would pass through the corner Q, where $x = 30, y = 0$.
Then the best solution is to have no machines of type 2, and this employs only 30 people, less than the capacity of the factory, but produces 1200 gloppits.
The best that can be done employing all 50 people is the previous solution P: $x = 10, y = 20$, producing only 800 gloppits.

3e CATTLE GRID

The pattern is

$$\begin{array}{ccc} 4 & 7 & 4 \\ 4 & & 7 \\ 7 & 4 & 4 \end{array}$$

or this pattern turned around.
(Again some algebra helps to reduce the possibilities.
If a and b are the two numbers involved then the numbers across the top of the pattern total $2a + b$, and also across the bottom, making $4a + 2b$ so far. The centre two numbers must be different to get an odd total (41) so

$$5a + 3b = 41.$$

Experiment produces $a = 4, b = 7$ and now it's not too hard to find the pattern.)

Some entrants were unable to accommodate all 41 cows and concluded that one was so close under the windows that the farmer couldn't see it!

4a PENTOMINOES

The full set of shapes made from five squares is as follows, starting with the three on the sheet:

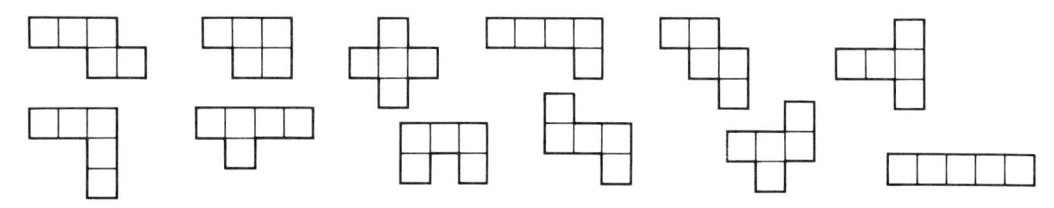

Of these, Jack can make nos 1, 2, 4, 6, 7 and 12, while Jill can make nos 1, 2, 4, 5, 8, 9, 10 and 11.
Neither can make the cross.

4b CHILD'S PLAY

Good old trial and error is probably the best approach here, guided by a little logic.
Write the sum as

$$\begin{array}{ccc} & A & A \\ B & A & C \\ B & A & A \\ \hline C & C & B \end{array}$$

Then from the hundreds column, $B = 1, 2, 3$ or 4.
When $B = 1, C = 2, 3$ or 4 and only $C = 3$ fits the units column, making $A = 4$ or 9. But $A = 9$ doesn't fit the tens column.
Likewise when $B = 2, C = 4, 5$ or 6 and this time $C = 4, A = 4$ or 9 and $C = 6$, $A = 3$ or 8 all fit the units column but only $C = 6, A = 8$ fits the tens column (also $A = C = 4$ is not allowed).
The cases $B = 3, B = 4$ don't give any solutions, so the only possibilities are

$$\begin{array}{cc} 44 & 88 \\ 143 \quad \text{and} & 286 \\ 144 & 288 \\ \hline 331 & 662 \end{array}$$

4c OH BOY!

The number 1985 is expressible in just two ways as the sum of two squares, as a little bit of experimentation shows.
In fact
$$1985 = 31^2 + 32^2 = 44^2 + 7^2.$$

Only the first of these fits the question. So Brenda's photograph of Boy George is 32 cm square and Bill's is 31 cm square.

4d BREAD LINE

This is an example of a problem where you can start at any position and steadily improve it to give the (unique) best position.
Starting at any crossroads, move so that the total of the distances decreases at each step. Note that you do not need to know the spacing of the streets for this purpose.
For example, moving from A to B decreases the total of the distances by the length of AB.

You end up at O, the best site for the bakery.

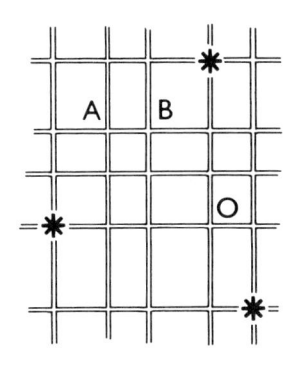

4e GREAT LITTLE ESCAPES

Five buses are needed.
Each spends 15 minutes at Speke and 5 minutes at Walton.

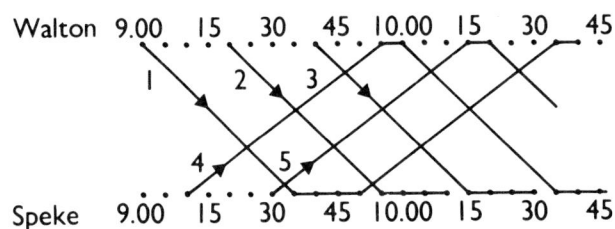

5a SCENIC ROUTE

There are several solutions.
In the solution illustrated (where the roads have been straightened out) the route can begin and end at any point of the circuit.

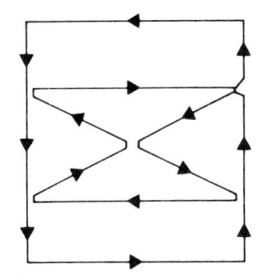

5b FAIR SQUARES

365 can be expressed as the sum of two squares in exactly two ways:
$$365 = 19^2 + 2^2 = 13^2 + 14^2$$

The sizes of the other squares were 13×13 and 14×14.

5c MORE FROM LESS

The only number less than 365 that can be expressed as the sum of two squares in three ways is 325. In fact
$$325 = 18^2 + 1^2 = 17^2 + 6^2 = 15^2 + 10^2.$$

5d PUT-UP JOB

The lowest total is provided by

> Gymnasium: Farretts
> Library: Winclough
> Dining Hall: Barreys.

The total is £144,000.

5e MR. M. Y. OPIA

There are 9 ways of putting all 4 letters in the wrong envelope.

The following reasoning reveals more than the question asks for.
For *two* letters and *two* envelopes there is clearly just one 'derangement' – an arrangement where no letter goes into the right envelope.
For *three* letters and *three* envelopes there are two derangements.
Now think of the case at hand of *four* letters – call them A, B, C, D and *four* envelopes – call them in correct order a, b, c, d. Then D is in a, b, or c: three cases. In each case there are two possibilities; take D in a for example.
  (i) If A is in d then letters B and C are also 'deranged', and as noted above there is only one way this can be done.
  (ii) If A is not in d then the three letters A, B, C are 'deranged' between envelopes b, c, d, and this can be done in two ways, as noted above.

So there are $3(1 + 2) = 9$ derangements of 4 letters.
The same argument shows that for 5 letters there are

$$4(2 + 9) = 44$$

derangements. Generally the derangements for n letters are
$$n[(\text{number for } n - 2) + (\text{number for } n - 1)]$$

A curious feature of the derangements is that the chance of the letters being deranged if the letters are put at random into envelopes approaches 0·36788 ..... (about 37 percent) as n gets larger. (0·36788 ... is actually $1/e$).

6a FOUR-MINUTE KILOMETRE

The cyclist takes three minutes to ride the 600 metres uphill, and one minute to ride the 400 metres downhill.

6b CUBICLES

The solution is $6^3 = 5^3 + 4^3 + 3^3$.

The first ten cubes are 1, 8, 27, 64, 125, 216, 343, 512, 729 and 1000.
Look for numbers $a > b > c > d$ with $a^3 - b^3 = c^3 + d^3$.
Start with $a = 10, b = 9$. Then look for c, d with $8 \geq c > d$ and
$c^3 + d^3 = 10^3 - 9^3 = 271$, and fail.
Then try $a = 10, b = 8$ and look for c, d with $7 \geq c > d$ and
$c^3 + d^3 = 10^3 - 8^3 = 488$, and fail again.
There is no point in trying $a = 10, b = 7$ because $10^3 - 7^3 > 6^3 + 5^3$.
So try $9^3 - 8^3 = 217 = c^3 + d^3 = 216 + 1$, which is the solution.
You also find $9^3 = 8^3 + 6^3 + 1^3$, but that violates the conditions of the problem.

6c GOING, GOING, GONE!

The doll costs £18 to start with, is reduced to £9 the first week, to £6 the second week, and to £5 the third and final week of the sale.
The later reductions are not fractions of the initial price but of the various reduced prices.

6d HOBSON'S ICES

The first flavour can be taken along with any of the twenty (including the first). Forgetting flavour no. 1, the second one can be taken with any of the remaining nineteen, and so on, giving

$$20 + 19 + 18 + \ldots + 3 + 2 + 1 = 210$$

as the total number of varieties. The trick way to add these numbers is

$$\begin{array}{l} 20 + 19 + 18 + \ldots + 3 + 2 + 1 \\ + 1 + 2 + 3 + \ldots + 18 + 19 + 20 \end{array} = 20 \times 21$$

by pairing the numbers vertically. But this is twice the number we want, which is therefore $\frac{1}{2} \times 20 \times 21 = 210$, as we said.

You can also work out that there are $\frac{1}{2} \times 20 \times 19 = 190$ choices with two *different* flavours, and 20 choices where you have a double scoop of one flavour. This makes $190 + 20 = 210$ in all.

6e VANDALISED STONES

You must do at least four hard jumps, as shown.

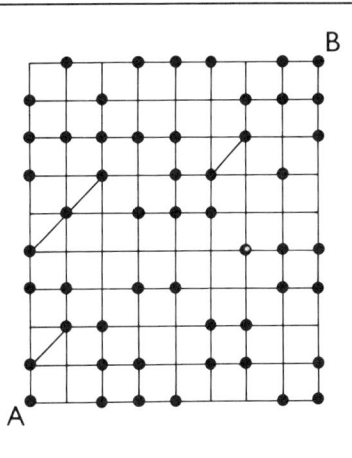

7a STARTHERE

The answer is 180°.
You could get this by direct measurement, but it is natural to ask whether the same answer is true for any five-pointed star, no matter how 'squint'.
This is in fact the case. The simplest proof is to lay a ruler along one arm of the star, say the horizontal one, and then turn it through each of the five angles in turn.
When one has done this the ruler will have turned through 180°, pointing in the opposite direction to its starting direction.

There are also various proofs based on the fact that the sum of the angles of a triangle is two right angles and of the angles of a pentagon is six right angles.

7b BOOKSALE

Let the first book cost £x. Then the last one costs £$(x + 12)$ and the middle one £$(x + 6)$, and either $x + 12 = x + 6 + x + 6\frac{1}{2}$, implying that $x + 12 = 2x + 12\frac{1}{2}$, that is, that $0 = x + \frac{1}{2}$, which clearly is not possible, or $x + 12 = x + 6 + x + 5\frac{1}{2}$, implying that $x + 12 = 2x + 11\frac{1}{2}$, that is, that $\frac{1}{2} = x$, implying that the cost of the first book is 50p.

Finally one has to compute $(1 + 2 + 3 + \ldots + 25)50\text{p}$.
Now

$$\begin{array}{l} 1 + 2 + 3 + \ldots + 24 + 25 \\ + 25 + 24 + 23 + \ldots + 2 + 1 \end{array} = (25)(26),$$

by pairing the numbers vertically. So

$$1 + 2 + 3 + \ldots + 24 + 25 = \tfrac{1}{2}(25)(26).$$

So the total cost of the books is £$\tfrac{1}{2}(25)(26)$ = £162.50.

7c BREAK BLOCK

Twenty-three breaks are required, no matter how the block is broken.
You were told in the question that each break makes two pieces from one, so you aren't allowed to break two or more pieces at the same time.
The answer has to be 23, because each break increases the number of pieces by one.

7d BIRTHDAY GIRLS

Louise is 15 and Tina is 24, for it is Louise who is the teenager, not Tina!
In fact nine years ago Louise was 6 (which is one quarter of 24) while Tina was 14, which is the same age as Louise is now.

You can do this one by trial and error, after you have sorted out the meaning of the words, or you can do it by algebra.
For example, let L be Louise's age in years and let x be the difference in years between Tina's age and Louise's age. Then Tina's age in years is $L + x$, while x years ago Tina's age was L and Louise's age was $L - x$.
Now we are told that $L + x = 4(L - x)$; that is that $5x = 3L$.
This is only possible if L is a multiple of 5. But Louise is a teenager. So $L = 15$. Then $x = 9$ and $T = 24$.
The solution $L = 10, T = 18$ won't do, as one is not a teenager at 10 years old.

7e ISLAND MAGIC

An Ass may leave Westminster and arrive at Midland in the form of a Bear.

A Bear may leave Westminster and arrive at Midland in the form of an Ass.

A Camel leaving Westminster is transformed on its first island and eaten on its second.

So the only animals which arrive at Midland are Asses and Bears.

8a BELT UP

The diagram shows the answer.
Since the inner pulleys have half the circumference of the outer ones (they have half the radius) the third pulley from the left rotates at half the speed of the one driving it. Of course the crossed-over belt makes the next one rotate anticlockwise.

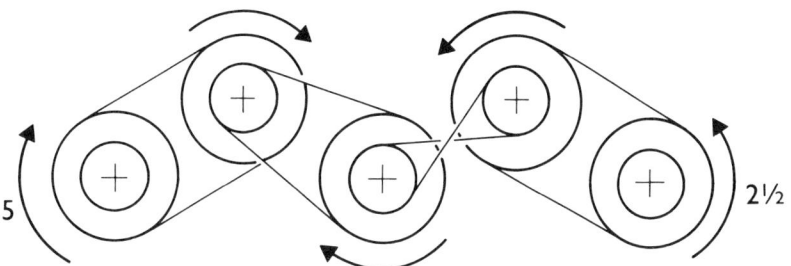

8b LOGIC

There is no choice as to which letter goes on which face.
There has to be an E opposite the E and an M on each of the other two faces.
Then, in each of the eight possible views of the cube with three faces showing, one of the E's is visible and two of the M's.
One might have some argument as to which way up each letter is placed.
We are not sure what the ideal solution should be to that!

8c BEAST OF BURDEN

The loads would be equally distributed if there was a total of 73 lb on each side. But this cannot be achieved.
The best possible is to have
$$7 + 11 + 19 + 37 = 74 \text{ lb}$$
on one side and to have
$$23 + 49 = 72 \text{ lb}$$
on the other.

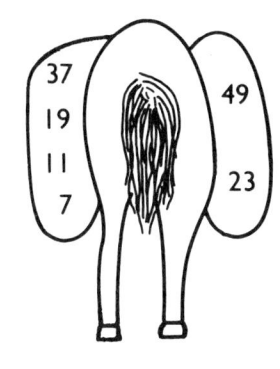

8d SECOND RATE

There are just two possibilities:

$100 = 38 + 38 + 24$, giving a second class total of $28 + 28 + 18 = 74$p*/*

and

$100 = 38 + 31 + 31$, giving a second class total of $28 + 22 + 22 = 72$p.

8e PLAN FOR REDUNDANCY

Yes, you can get to every street from A.

No, you cannot leave from every street.
The loop C will not let you escape.

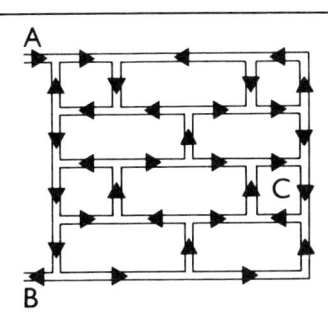

9a THE RIGHT TIMES

The neatest way to do this is to consider times when the hands are *together* (angle 0°). This occurs at 12 o'clock and thereafter every $\frac{12}{11}$ hours (since the minute hand moves relative to the hour hand $330° = \frac{11}{12} \times 360°$ in one hour). Between any two successive times when the hands are together they are twice at right angles. So in 24 hours they are at right angles

$$2 \times \frac{24}{12/11} = 44 \text{ times.}$$

Notice that the same reasoning applies to any angle, not just a right angle. There will be 44 occasions on which the hands make any given angle except 0° or 180°. For these there are 22 occasions.

9b SUPER SHELL

Steve wins by a quarter section.

Ignore the middle section, as both go the same speed in that part. If Steve takes time 2 units over the first and third sections, then Seb takes time $\frac{1}{2}$ unit over the first section and 2 units over the third, so finishes $\frac{1}{2}$ unit of time behind, that is, a quarter section behind.

9c ANNELID vs GASTROPOD

Steven and the worm are together four times altogether – at the start, and after Steve has done 2, 4 or 6 laps.

9d MR. COMPOST

This question can be solved by trial and error but a little algebra helps enormously. With x rhododendrons, y roses and z bedding plants,

$$5x + y + \frac{1}{20}z = 100 \quad (\text{cost} = £100)$$

$$x + y + z = 100 \quad (100 \text{ plants}).$$

Subtracting, $4x - \frac{19}{20}z = 0$, that is $\frac{x}{z} = \frac{19}{80}$ since we know x and z are not zero. So the smallest solution is $x = 19, z = 80$ ($\frac{19}{80}$ is in its lowest terms) giving $y = 1$. The next solution, $x = 38$ and $z = 160$, is too big. Admittedly 19 rhododendrons, 1 rose and 80 bedding plants is an extraordinary combination!

9e TEAM WORK

There are 105 different ways for the youngsters to enrol.
Clearly they have to be split into a three and two twos, but this is the start of the problem, not the finish.
If you make a list you will find that there are

$$35 (= 15 + 10 + 6 + 3 + 1)$$

ways of choosing the trio.
In each case there are then three different ways in which the remaining four can be paired off (not six, as some children said), giving $105 = 35 \times 3$ ways in all.
We considered the order of the three groups not to be relevant.

ABC				
ABD				
ABE				
ABF				
ABG				
ACD	BCD			
ACE	BCE			
ACF	BCF			
ACG	BCG			
ADE	BDE	CDE		
ADF	BDF	CDF		
ADG	BDG	CDG		
AEF	BEF	CEF	DEF	
AEG	BEG	CEG	DEG	
AFG	BFG	CFG	DFG	EFG

10a INSURANCE ANGLE

Since there are 26 letters and 10 digits there are 36 symbols, so the angle between any two adjacent ones must be 10°, since there are 360 degrees in a full circle. Starting with the arrow pointing to R one has to turn through

$$30° + 100° + 120° + 110° = 360°.$$
$$R \to O \to Y \to A \to L$$

The answer is therefore 360°.

10b GRANNIE'S SECRET

This is easily solved by trial and error, starting with numbers around 70.
Alternatively it can be done by algebra:
The two ages are a, b where
$a^2 - b^2 = (a - b)(a + b) = 1988 = 2 \times 2 \times 7 \times 71$.
So $a - b$ is part of this product and $a + b$ is the rest.
The only possibility for $a + b$ is 2×71, the others being too big or too small for grandparents!
So $a + b = 2 \times 71$, $a - b = 2 \times 7$ and these give $a = 78, b = 64$.

So Grannie is 78 and Grandpa is 64.

10c BEST FRIEND

Chris is a friend of each of the other four.

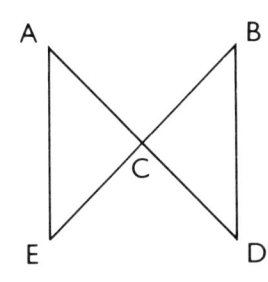

10d SPACE INVADERS

The first part is relatively easy – the 46 antennae must come from 5 males, with 5 antennae each and 3 females with 7 antennae each.

The *five* possible ways of making up 140 are

$$28M, 21M + 5F, 14M + 10F, 7M + 15F, 20F.$$

10e POSTAL ORDER

The arrangement shown is, in fact, the unique worst one, with 1 in the given position; that is, the sum

$$(5 - 1) + (3 - 2) + (4 - 2) + (5 - 4) + (5 - 2) + (5 - 3) + (4 - 1) = 16$$

is the highest possible. There is just one arrangement (shown) giving sum 10, and that is the lowest possible.

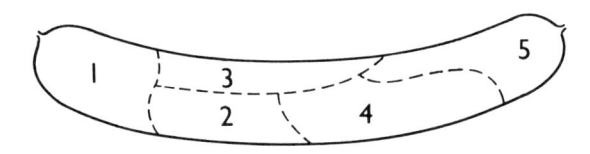

Three arrangements give sum 11.

1a MAGIC IT

The only solution is shown on the right.

For if the 4 is changed to $4 + x$ then the 10, 2 and 8 must be changed to $10 + x$, $2 + x$ and $8 + x$ to keep the sums of the outer horizontal and vertical lines the same. But then there is no possible way of filling in the middle square, for to keep the sums of the horizontal and vertical lines correct the 6 would have to be changed to $6 - x$, while to keep the diagonal sums correct it would have to be changed to $6 + x$, and one cannot have it both ways.

5	4	9
10	6	2
3	8	7

1b PRESENTS A PROBLEM

The easiest way to see this is to open out the cube by cutting along edges and lay the 6 square faces flat on the table.
A ribbon pasted flat on the cube will unfold so as to be straight on the flattened cube.

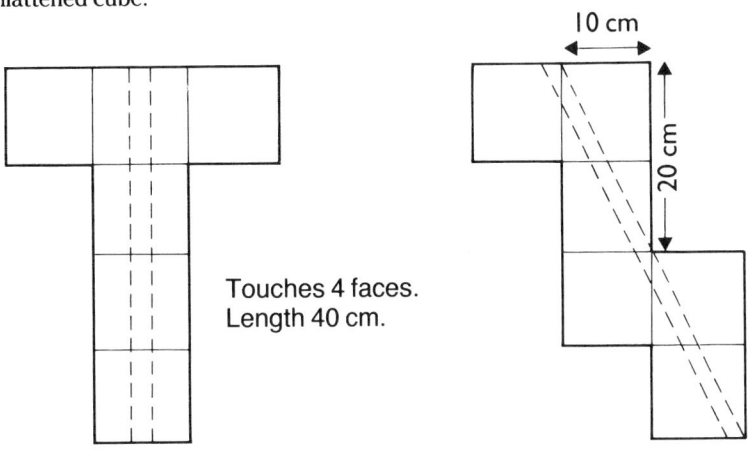

Touches 4 faces. Length 40 cm.

Touches all 6 faces. Length by measurement is about 44.7 cm, or exactly by Pythagoras' theorem is $2\sqrt{10^2 + 20^2} = 20\sqrt{5}$ cm.

1c IT'S A KNOCKOUT

Let m be the number of matches and b the number of byes at the first attempt. Then from what we are told it follows that $m + b = 32$ and that $m + 4 = b$, since there will have to be four more matches in the first round than the secretary first reckoned to take care of the four additional entries found.
From these equations it is not difficult to see that $m = 14$ and that $b = 18$. Therefore the total number of competitors is

$$2m + b + 4 = 28 + 18 + 4 = 50.$$

1d BUSY BEES

A little thought shows that in passing from one day to the next, a multiple of 6 is always added to the number of cells.
First 6, then 12, then 18, and so on are added.
Thus at the end of the sixth day there are

$1 + 6 + 12 + 18 + 24 + 30 = 91$ cells.

It is not difficult to go on to calculate the number of cells after $7, 8, \ldots$ days and to discover that after 19 days there are 1027 cells and that the number 1000 is passed during the 19th day.
Incidentally the general formula after n days takes the pleasant form

$$\text{Number of cells} = n^3 - (n - 1)^3.$$

© OUP 1990. This page may be reproduced for class use within the purchaser's institute

1e REVOLUTIONARY

The Geneva Wheel rotates anticlockwise, but moves only when the peg on the crank is moving up or down one of the six slots.
The circular part of the crank locks the Geneva Wheel and stops it moving while the peg is moved round on the crank from one slot to the next.
The axles of both wheels are of course in fixed positions all the time.

2a CHIMPS ARE CHAMPS

One systematic approach is to draw up a table in which the individual game scores are recorded. This is done below, where the Chimps' three scores are in the first row, the Wombats' in the second row, and so on.
The row and column totals are read off from the league table which is given.
The zero sums mean of course that all entries in that row or column are zero.
It is an easy matter to fill in the remaining numbers.
In fact, you can even work out the full table without knowing the Lion-Zebra score!

Thus the six scores are:
- Chimps v. Wombats   0 : 0
- Chimps v. Zebras   2 : 1
- Chimps v. Lions   3 : 0
- Wombats v. Zebras   0 : 0
- Wombats v. Lions   0 : 0
- Zebras v. Lions   1 : 1

	C	W	Z	L	
C	–	0	2	3	5
W	0	–	0	0	0
Z	1	0	–	1	2
L	0	0	1	–	1
	1	0	3	4	

2b INSECTICIDE

The bugs can trap the insect even if the insect is not stupid!
One way is as follows:

Fastbug begins by getting on to side BC while slowbug stays at D.
So long as slowbug stays there the insect is wise to keep clear of BD and CD.
Since fastbug can get from B to C directly in the time it takes the insect to get from B to C via A, fastbug is soon able to prevent the insect passing B or C at all. Once this is so, slowbug then moves painfully from D to A, after which the insect gets trapped either on AB or on AC.

There is of course nothing in the way the question is worded to prevent any of the creatures changing direction at any time.

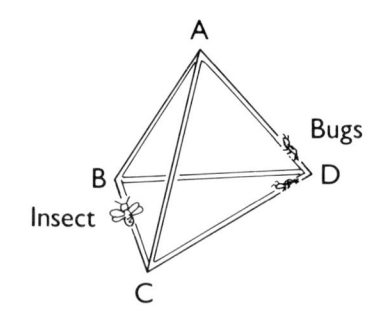

2c COGGLY

When A rises 1 cm a certain number of teeth of A will engage with the cog next to A, the same number of this cog with D and the same number of D with B.
D moves anticlockwise and raises B by the same distance, 1 cm.

All cogs except D have 8 teeth and D has 16 teeth, twice as many.
So if E moves clockwise 20°, then D moves anticlockwise only 10° but C moves anticlockwise 20°.

2d TWICE TWO

This beautiful question actually arose in the practical situation of using a copying machine with a maximum magnification of 1.4 to exactly double the size of a document! But nobody could think of a wording which made the question both short and intelligible, so it ended up as a purely numerical question. The most systematic solution involves multiplying every decimal by 100, and therefore the 2 by 1,000,000. That is, we look for factorizations

$$1?? \times 1?? \times 1?? = 2\,000\,000.$$

The only suitable factorization of $2\,000\,000$ is $125 \times 125 \times 128$, so the only solution is $1.25 \times 1.25 \times 1.28$.

2e FINAL CHALLENGE

The pattern is a 'Pascal triangle' – one where if, as in the diagram, there are x ways to reach X and y ways to reach Y, then there are $x + y$ ways to reach Z.

Also there is just one way to reach any point on either the NW or the SW edge. If one starts at the Western corner and assigns to each letter in turn the number of ways in which it can be reached, working steadily from West to East, the three numbers asked for quickly come out to be 3, 4 and 70, respectively.

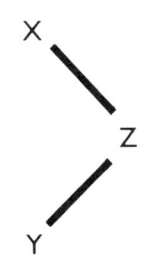

3a PLOT PLANTS

The secret of this question is to realize that the numbers in the middle squares of opposite sides must add up to $20 - 7 - 7 = 6$.
Now, given that there are to be at most four trees in each square, there are just two different ways in which this can be done, namely 2 and 4, and 3 and 3. The possible solutions, up to rotations and reflections, are then as follows:

4	2	1
2		4
1	4	2

3	2	2
2		4
2	4	1

2	3	2
3		3
2	3	2

1	3	3
3		3
3	3	1

3	2	2
3		3
1	4	2

There are four cases really, since the second and fifth both involve the same numbers, namely 1, 2, 3 and 4. If one was allowed to plant up to five trees in any given square then there are three further cases, namely

5	1	1
1		5
1	5	1

4	2	1
1		5
2	4	1

3	3	1
1		5
3	3	1

3b SQUARE ROUTES

The possible ways through the maze are as follows:

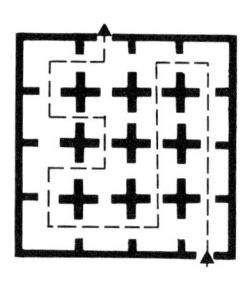

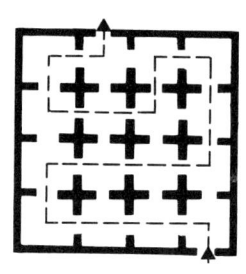

or any of these four routes, including the one in the question, but run in the reverse direction.

If the door at the top is into the left-hand compartment there is no route. The crafty way to see this is to think of the sixteen squares as being part of a chessboard. Then one sees that one has to visit 'black' and 'white' squares alternately, with the last square necessarily being of opposite colour to the first.
But the top left and bottom right squares must be of the same colour.
So no path is possible.

3c DIG THIS

The treasure lies on the perpendicular bisector of BC.
To find the position on this line it is probably easiest to just measure.
It is approximately 0.95 cm (on the map!) from the cliff edge, although another position, some 2 cm out to sea, fits the data also but is ruled out for other reasons.

3d COUNTER FEAT

Including the $\frac{1}{2}$ second pause at the end of each number, Ultravox takes 1 second to read a one digit number, and there are 9 of these, takes $1\frac{1}{2}$ seconds to read a 2-digit number, and there are 90 of these, takes 2 seconds to read a 3-digit number, and there are 900 of these, takes $2\frac{1}{2}$ seconds to read a 4-digit number, and there are 9000 of these, takes 3 seconds to read a 5-digit number, and there are 90 000 of these, and takes $3\frac{1}{2}$ seconds to read a 6-digit number, and there are 900 000 of these. Finally there is one 7-digit number, namely 1 000 000, which takes a final $3\frac{1}{2}$ seconds. So the total time spent by Ultravox in reciting the numbers is

$$9 + 90 \times 1\frac{1}{2} + 900 \times 2 + 9000 \times 2\frac{1}{2} + 90000 \times 3 + 900000 \times 3\frac{1}{2} + 3\frac{1}{2} \text{ seconds,}$$

which works out at $34\,444\,447\frac{1}{2}$ seconds, which is 57407 minutes, to the nearest minute, which is 957 hours, to the nearest hour, which is 40 days to the nearest day.

3e DRINK PROBLEM

The number of quarter cups filled with milk is $2 + 1 + 1 + 1 + 0 = 5$ and the number of quarter cups filled with coffee is $2 + 3 + 3 + 3 + 4 = 15$, three times as much. So all the milk is used and three-quarters of the coffee.
The coffee jug is left one quarter full.

4a DAVY JONES'S LOCKER

With repetitions allowed there are fifteen possibilities for the first three digits of the locker number, namely

$$004, 013, 022, 031, 040,$$
$$103, 112, 121, 130,$$
$$202, 211, 220,$$
$$301, 310,$$
$$400,$$

only the six permutations of 013 being relevant if the alternative interpretation is adopted. With repetitions allowed there are also fifteen possibilities for the last two digits, namely

$$01, 02, 03, 04, 05,$$
$$12, 13, 14, 15,$$
$$23, 24, 25,$$
$$34, 35,$$
$$45,$$

while if they are disallowed there are just three, namely 24, 25, 45.

Putting these together we find that if repetitions are allowed then there are $15 \times 15 = 225$ possibilities in all, while if this is not the case then there are only $6 \times 3 = 18$ possibilities.

4b RAFFLE BAFFLER

Multiples of $1, 2, 3, \ldots, 10$ will be multiples of $5 \times 7 \times 8 \times 9 = 2520$ (this is the lowest common multiple of $1, 2, 3, \ldots, 10$).
So the sum of the ticket numbers is either 2520 or 5040 or 7560 (the sum is never over 10,000 since the top ticket number is 2000).

The sum is always 5 times the middle ticket since
$(n-2) + (n-1) + n + (n+1) + (n+2) = 5n$.
So the middle ticket is $\frac{1}{5}(2520) = 504$ or $\frac{1}{5}(5040) = 1008$ or $\frac{1}{5}(7560) = 1512$.

But middle tickets end in 3 or 8, so the winning number is 1008.

4c ROOMS WITH A VIEW

There are many solutions, one being

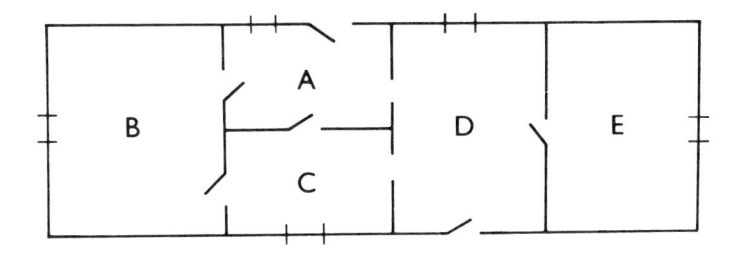

but the bungalow need not be rectangular overall.
Besides the doors and windows prescribed, one would imagine that the architect would add at least a front door and possibly a back door as well.

4d ADVERSE CONDITIONS

Eleven trains get through per hour, the number using each section of track being indicated in the revised diagram, which shows also the direction in which each section of track is run. The key is to arrange things so that the same number of trains enter each node of the network as leave it.

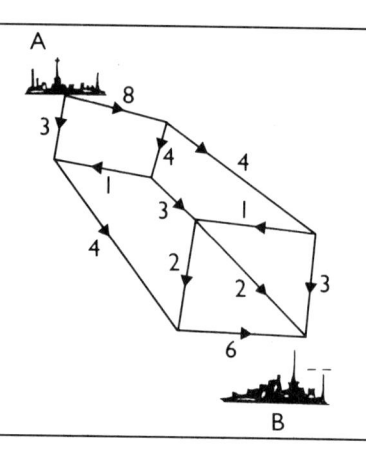

4e ESCALATION

The correct answer is 27. The escalator has moved 18 steps while Peter climbs, by which time Ann has climbed half of 36, namely 18. So Ann is climbing as fast as the escalator.

So by the time Ann has climbed 27 steps the escalator has carried her a further 27, and she is at the top.

5a PLOTTING AND PLANNING

A B C D	A B C D	A B C D	A B C D
B A D C	B C D A	B A D C	B D A C
C D A B	C D A B	C D B A	C A D B
D C B A	D A B C	D C A B	D C B A

These are called 'Latin squares'. The enumeration of these 4 possibilities is easy, starting from the fact that the square adjacent to the two B's must be A, C or D.

If it is A then the second line is BADC; if C then it is BCDA; if D then it is BDAC, etc.

(In the originally set question we only specified that *adjacent* plots going up or down or across were to have different treatments.

This inadvertent error opened the door to rather a lot of alternative solutions: there are 2834 in all, as we discovered after covering several sheets of paper doing the enumeration. So we can challenge you to show that this is the right number!)

5b FOUR SQUARE

Working backwards, and knowing that after the final transaction

  A has £16, B has £16, C has £16 and D has £16,

it follows that at the previous stage, before Dan doubles Albert,

  A has £8, B has £16, C has £16 and D has £24.

At the stage before that, before Chris doubles Dan,

  A has £8, B has £16, C has £28 and D has £12.

One stage earlier, before Brenda doubles Chris,

  A has £8, B has £30, C has £14 and D has £12.

So, finally, at the outset, before Albert doubles Brenda,

  A has £23, B has £15, C has £14 and D has £12.

A prudent check of this result is to note that the initial amounts that we have worked out do indeed total to £64.

5c SUM HOW

A little bit of experimentation should convince you that there must either be carrying only in the 'hundreds' column, as in the picture, or else there must be carrying in each column, in which case 9 has to be in the units column. There are in fact six basic solutions, namely

$$\begin{array}{cccccc} 623 & 342 & 473 & 264 & 246 & 437 \\ 475 & 756 & 589 & 789 & 789 & 589 \\ \hline 1098 & 1098 & 1062 & 1053 & 1035 & 1026 \end{array}$$

from each of which fifteen others can be obtained by swapping numbers between the first row and the second or by interchanging the tens and units columns in the first two cases or the hundreds and tens columns in the other four. This gives 96 solutions in all.

We were very happy if the children found a reasonable variety of these, and most gained marks for finding at least a few.

5d CARTOGRAPHY

The sign-post illustrating this question was at Downside, and the road across the island was only two miles long, from Downside to Aberavon.
The five towns must have been related as in the accompanying map, with Coldharbour duly at the North end and Eastward Ho on the Eastern side.

(Of course, the roads need not be straight.)

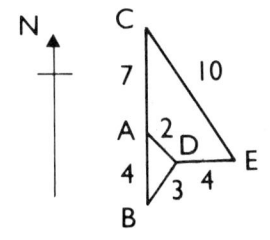

5e ON THE CARDS

The factorization of 90 is $2 \times 3 \times 3 \times 5$.
The only ways of factorizing 90 into a product of *three* factors, one of which can be 1 but none of which can be as big as 15, are

$$\begin{array}{ll} 1 \times 9 \times 10 & \text{adding up to } 20 \\ 2 \times 5 \times 9 & 16 \\ 3 \times 5 \times 6 & 14 \\ 3 \times 3 \times 10 & 16 \end{array}$$

Since it was *not* possible to work out the ages the number of cards on the mantelpiece must have been 16.
(With 20 or 14 cards you can deduce immediately that the ages are 1, 9, 10 or 3, 5, 6 respectively.)

6a JOB OPPORTUNITIES

Since the largest number occurring is 9 and there is no 8 in the last column we must have $9 + 9 + 8 + 7 + 7$ or $9 + 9 + 8 + 8 + 6$ or $9 + 8 + 8 + 8 + 7$ to get a total of 40. The two 9's must be C1 and G3 and this leads only to CBGDH. With one 9 it could only be C1, since the 7 in the last column belongs to G who has the other two 9's.
This leads to CHBDG, CBEDG or CHEDG, giving 4 solutions in all.

6b CLOSE ENCOUNTERS

At 8 am	$1 + 3 = 4$	people know the news
8.10	$4 + 3^2 = 13$	"
8.20	$13 + 3^3 = 40$	"
8.30	$40 + 3^4 = 121$	"
8.40	$121 + 3^5 = 364$	"
8.50	$364 + 3^6 = 1093$	"
9.00	$1093 + 3^7 = 3280$	"

Notice that you have to add the previous number to a power of 3, not just take a power of 3. So by 9 am, 3279 inhabitants know the news, which is more than half of 6000.

6c ACROSS THE BOARD

Instead of counting routes from the top left to the bottom right we can count them from *any* square to the bottom right, and then a pattern emerges.
In fact if the block shown on the right occurs anywhere, where a, b, c are the numbers of routes from that square to the bottom right, then it's easy to convince yourself that the blank square has $a + b + c$ routes. (If we excluded diagonal moves then of course it would be just $a + c$.) Now the whole pattern can be built up:

```
63  25  7  1
25  13  5  1
 7   5  3  1
 1   1  1  1
```

This gives the answer 63.
(For a 5×5 board the answer is 321; for 6×6 it is 1683; for 7×7 it is 8989, for 8×8 it is 48639. Can anyone find a general formula?)

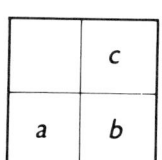

6d WRAP UP

9" by 9" is too small, since $81 < 96$.
But 11" by 11" will do, provided that the book is laid diagonally on the paper. We expect a mainly experimental approach, but here is a discussion of the geometry.

Consider a thin rectangular book of size $b \times c$ placed diagonally on a square piece of paper of size $a \times a$ (that is, with the sides of the rectangle parallel to the diagonals of the square). See the upper diagram. The condition for the rectangle to fit at all works out to be $a\sqrt{2} \geq b + c$ (that is, the diagonal of the square must be at least as long as half the perimeter of the rectangle). Can you prove this using Pythagoras' theorem? Rather remarkably, if the rectangle fits diagonally, then the paper can always be folded over to cover the upper surface of the rectangle. This is easiest to see when the rectangle *just* fits (lower diagram), and the general case follows from this.

For with $b \leq c$ it is fairly easy to check that the shaded flaps, after folding, cover at least one quarter of the rectangle provided that $a\sqrt{2} \geq 2b$, but this is assured by $a\sqrt{2} \geq b + c \geq 2b$. Note that, after folding, the edges PQ and QR lie along the same horizontal line.

For $b = 6, c = 8$, the condition $a\sqrt{2} \geq b + c$ gives $a \geq \sqrt{98}$, slightly less than 10, so for a *very* thin book $a = 10$ would do, but $a = 11$ is safer. Incidentally, granted that the paper does wrap the rectangle, it must follow that the area of the paper is at least twice the area of the rectangle, that is that $a^2 \geq 2bc$. How does this follow from $a\sqrt{2} \geq b + c$?

You may already have wondered whether by slanting the book away from the diagonal of the square a larger rectangle can be covered.
Can a square of size less than $\sqrt{98}$ ever wrap a 6×8 (thin!) book?

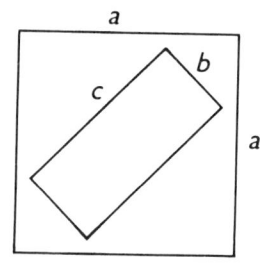

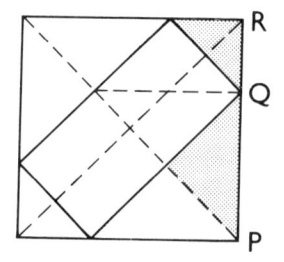

6e WIND BAND

Leslie cannot be the angler and neither can David, so the angler is Gareth.
Thus Gareth is not the trombone player; also he is not the clarinettist.
Hence Gareth plays the flute. Now we deduce that Leslie plays the clarinet
and David the trombone.
(But there is no way of telling which of David and Leslie is the swimmer!)

7a FAIR PLAY

Dave's score of $120 = 40 + 5 \times 16$;
Karen's score of $110 = 2 \times 23 + 4 \times 16$;
Steve's score of $100 = 4 \times 17 + 2 \times 16$.

In fact the information that the bull is hit only once is redundant.

7b SEXTUPLETS

The number 6 can be subdivided in *eleven* ways, namely

6, 5 + 1, 4 + 2, 4 + 1 + 1, 3 + 3,
3 + 2 + 1 (as in the picture),
3 + 1 + 1 + 1, 2 + 2 + 2, 2 + 2 + 1 + 1,
2 + 1 + 1 + 1 and 1 + 1 + 1 + 1 + 1 + 1.

(This problem celebrated the birth of the Walton sextuplets on Merseyside.)

7c METRIC RULES

When using small marks, four of them are enough and there are fourteen
ways of doing it. Seven of these are by putting the marks at the following
number of centimetres from one end:

$$1, 4, 5, 10 \quad 1, 2, 3, 8 \quad 2, 5, 8, 11 \quad 2, 4, 5, 11$$
$$1, 5, 9, 11 \quad 3, 6, 10, 11 \quad 1, 3, 5, 11.$$

The other seven are obtained by subtracting the numbers from 12,
i.e. measuring from the other end.
So, for example, 1, 4, 5, 10 has as its twin 2, 7, 8, 11.
Using lines rather than marks, some competition entrants produced the
following solution using only three lines.

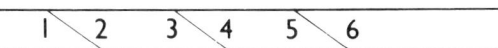

7d HIC!

There seems to be little alternative to trial and error in a problem of this kind. The solution can be displayed by showing after each step the contents of the 3 containers:

13 pt.	11 pt.	5 pt.
0	11	0
0	11	5
11	0	5
13	0	3
13	3	0
8	3	5
8	8	0

7e ACID TEST

This is surprisingly hard to visualize. There are 6 edges of the cube which do *not* pass through the suspension point or the opposite corner, and the new face will contain the mid-point of each of these 6 edges. In fact it is a regular hexagon, as in the figure where you are looking up at the new face and the dotted edges have dissolved. If the bottom corner of the cube is dipped just a little way into the acid then the new bottom face is an equilateral triangle. At what stage of lowering the cube does the new bottom face become six-sided? What does it look like when it has just become six-sided?

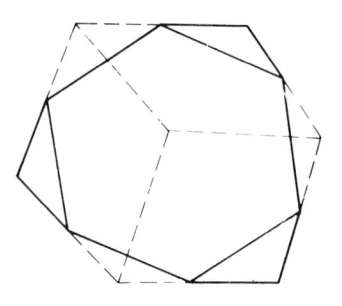

8a MARK THIS

The two marks that are lost can either be from any one of the six questions or one can be dropped from one of the six and the other from another, this being possible in $\frac{1}{2}(6 \times 5) = 15$ ways, giving 21 ways in all.

8b BALL POINTS

First of all we accept that, strictly speaking, a ball has no corners. However, the various squares and triangles do.
That being said, the only possibility is that the 'ball' looks like

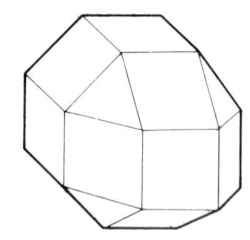

which has the 'symmetry of a cube'

and has 18 square faces (one for each of the eight faces of a cube and one for each of its twelve edges), 8 triangular faces (one for each corner of the cube), and $8 \times 3 = 24$ meeting points, there being exactly one corner of a triangle at each meeting point.

8c ANATHEMATICS

Let's write A for AAAG, B for BAA and S for SOG.
The 9 possible pairs are

AA, AB, AS, BA, BB, BS, SA, SB, SS.

For ease of writing, I'll spell out round the table clockwise by a list of letters starting with BSA. Remember the last one in the list then links up with the B at the start.

Somewhere there must be two S's side by side.
There are 5 places we can try:

1. BSASS1234
2. BSA1SS234
3. BSA12SS34
4. BSA123SS4
5. BSA1234SS

where 1, 2, 3, 4 are unknown letters.
We now try to fill 1, 2, 3, 4 and it's helpful to remember two A's and two B's must sit together somewhere.

1. SA, SS already there ∴ 1 = B to make sure SB happens. Sitting two B's together gives $\boxed{\text{BSASSBBAA}}$ or $\boxed{\text{BSASSBAAB}}$
2. BS, SS already there so 1 = A to give AS and 2 = B to give SB. Sitting two B's together gives $\boxed{\text{BSAASSBAB}}$ or $\boxed{\text{BSAASSBBA}}$
3. BS, SS already there so 2 = A to give AS and 3 = B to give SB. Now we can't fill in 1 so that just two A's sit together. They end up all together or none together, so we get no solution here.
4. This is similar to 2 and gives $\boxed{\text{BSAABASSB}}$ or $\boxed{\text{BSABAASSB}}$
5. Is similar to 1 and gives $\boxed{\text{BSABBAASS}}$ or $\boxed{\text{BSAABBASS}}$

So there are *eight* solutions in all.
(I wonder how they decided which one to adopt, especially since they all hated mathematics!)

8d CUBE ROUTES

This was tricky because some routes are entirely on the front, some are on the back, while others are partially on the front and partially on the back. The number of entirely visible routes is 24 but the total is neither twice this nor three times this!

There are three vertices immediately below the top one and by symmetry the same number of routes will start out to each of these three.
It simplifies the diagram to consider routes from only *one* of these three vertices, say the right-hand one in the diagram accompanying the question. For this purpose we can throw away half the cube, for none of these routes can lie on that. What remains is shown in the picture.

Arrows go downhill and we work our way up from the *bottom*, marking each vertex in turn with the number of routes to the bottom *starting at that vertex*. The rule is that each vertex is labelled with the sum of the numbers immediately below it. Then it quickly becomes clear that there are 18 routes.

This applies to each of the three vertices mentioned above so the total is 54 routes.

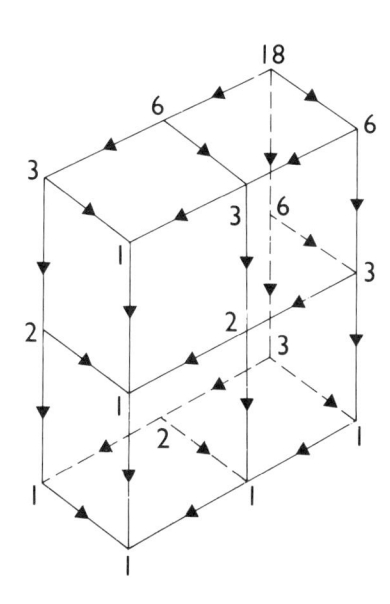

8e THE LAST ONE

Each domino has two *ends* and each end has a certain *number* of dots, either 0, 1, 2, 3, 4, 5, or 6, on it. The total number of ends with a given number of dots is eight: for example for 5 dots we have

$\boxed{5\ 0}$, $\boxed{5\ 1}$, $\boxed{5\ 2}$, $\boxed{5\ 3}$, $\boxed{5\ 4}$, $\boxed{5\ 5}$, $\boxed{5\ 6}$

in which there are eight 5's.

Suppose that certain dominoes have been laid down working to the right and that the number at the right-hand end of the last domino is *not* a 6.
Say it is a 4. Apart from that 4 the 4's in the line will occur in pairs, because of the way in which dominoes are laid down with ends having matching numbers.
Thus the number of 4's in the line will be *odd* and so will not be eight: there must be at least one 4 on an unused domino. So the line can be continued. (The same holds if the last domino to be laid down is a double-four.)
This applies so long as the right-hand end is not a 6, so when the line cannot be continued further *the right-hand end must be a 6.*

The same reasoning shows that if you work in both directions until you get stuck or use up all the dominoes then the numbers at the far left and right ends of the line will be the same.
If John finds that the ends of his line are not the same – maybe they are 2 and 5 – then he can say at once what the missing domino is – in this case it will be the $\boxed{2\ 5}$ *domino, BUT if the ends do match then he can only say that a double must be missing.*
He cannot say which one, since for instance a double-four could be fitted in between any two fours in the line.

1 CHAIN REACTION

After subtraction the middle digit is always 9 and the outer digits add up to 9. Thus the top number in the second column has digits of the form $9, a, 9 - a$, where $5 \leq a \leq 9$. (There is an exception: if you start with a number having three equal digits then subtraction gives 000, but this gives a very short chain.)

Subtracting again gives the digits $a - 1, 9, 10 - a$, which rearranged is $9, a - 1, 10 - a$ unless $a = 5$ when we have got 954 back again.

So the second digit at the top of each column decreases by 1 until it reaches 5, then stays put.

So the longest chain is obtained by arranging that $a = 9$, and this can be done by starting with a number like 776 or 766 where the largest and smallest digits differ by 1. The top lines of the columns are then

$$776 \quad 990 \quad 981 \quad 972 \quad 963 \quad 954 \quad 954$$

with *six different numbers in the chain*.

If you object to 099 as the result of the first subtraction then the best you can do is to start a number like 765:

$$765 \quad 981 \quad 972 \quad 963 \quad 954 \quad 954.$$

Here there are *five different numbers in the chain*.

With four-digit numbers you find every chain ends in 7641 and there are at most eight different numbers in the chain. Starting with, for example, 7652 gives eight different numbers.

Five-digit numbers? Not all chains end with the same number and there are 'cycles' this time. Try starting with 74943.

The numbers 954 and 7641 are called Kaprekar constants (for base 10), after their discoverer (1955). Or perhaps one of their discoverers, for B. A. Kordemsky, in his *Moscow puzzles*, first published in Russia in 1956 and in England by Pelican Books in 1975, gives the same problem in number 350 of the collection.

He ascribes the discovery of 7641 to one Y. N. Lambina.

Perhaps one day the same number will turn up in a lost manuscript of Isaac Newton!

The problem appeared in the 1980 CHALLENGE competition.
A recent reference for Kaprekar constants is M. E. Lines, *A number for your thoughts*, Adam Hilger Ltd, Bristol, 1986.

2 DOWNHILL ALL THE WAY

This problem, like many others, can be solved by intelligent trial and error.

The first part is solved by $12435 \{ \genfrac{}{}{0pt}{}{123}{45}$.

Among many possible solutions to the second part is $54321 \{ \genfrac{}{}{0pt}{}{531}{42}$,

$53142 \{ \genfrac{}{}{0pt}{}{512}{34}$, $51234 \{ \genfrac{}{}{0pt}{}{1234}{5}$.

The following technique works for any number of waggons and provides an interesting link with numbers in base 2. Let us write 0 for 'let the waggon roll into the North branch' and 1 for 'let the waggon roll into the South branch'. Then each waggon has associated with it a string of 0's and 1's.

Since the N branch is always cleared before the S branch, it is not very hard to convince yourself of the following. Treat the string of 0's and 1's as a single number written in base 2.

The base-2 digits, reading right to left, represent the fate of that particular waggon on the first, second, etc. moves. (For example, 010 is 2 and represents N, S, N; 110 is 6 and represents N, S, S.) The crucial observation is that waggon A ends up nearer to the engine than waggon B precisely when the base-2 number representing what happens to A is *less than* the base-2 number representing what happens to B, or else *equal to* this number and A was nearer the engine than B in the first place.

(If the numbers are *equal* then A and B do exactly the same thing so can't be reversed in order.) For instance, with 010 for A and 110 for B, A and B are treated the same on the first two moves and then on the third move A goes North and B goes South so A ends up nearer the engine than B.

To turn 41352 into 12345 using this, proceed as follows:

(1)	(2)	(3)	
4	2	10	Column (1) is the starting order.
1	0	00	In column (2), waggons 1 and 2 are already in the
3	1	01	correct relative position (1 to the left of 2) so label
5	2	10	them 0. They will get the same treatment.
2	0	00	Waggon 3 gets number 1: it's not in the correct position relative to 4 or 5. Waggons 4 and 5 are correct relative to each other so get number 2.

Column (3) is the base-2 expansion of (2).

Now the separate columns of (3) tell you what to do: $41352 \{ \genfrac{}{}{0pt}{}{4152}{3}$ from the last column of (3) and $41523 \{ \genfrac{}{}{0pt}{}{123}{45}$ from the other.

This is a different solution from that given above.
The table for starting with position 54321 is

5	4	100	and this gives the solution above.
4	3	011	
3	2	010	
2	1	001	
1	0	000	

3 + = ×

The only three whole numbers between 1 and 10 inclusive having the same sum as their product are 1, 2, 3.

There are three possibilities for five numbers.
These are 11125, 11133 and 11222.

Here is a systematic way to solve the first part.

Let a, b, c be the numbers in increasing size, that is $a \leq b \leq c$.

Try $a = 1$; then $abc = a + b + c$ gives

$$bc = 1 + b + c, \text{ that is } c = \frac{b+1}{b-1} = 1 + \frac{2}{b-1}.$$

Now try possibilities for b:

$b = 1$ is impossible;

$b = 2$ gives $c = 3$, which is a solution;

$b > 2$ gives $c < 2$, which is forbidden.

Next try $a = 2$. Then $2bc = 2 + b + c$, that is $c = \frac{b+2}{2b-1}$.

Try possibilities for b: $b = 2, 3, 4, \ldots$.

Then we have $c = \frac{4}{3}, \frac{5}{5}, \frac{6}{7}, \ldots$;

so c is never as big as 2, which contradicts $c \geq b$.

Thus $a, b, c = 1, 2, 3$ is the only possibility.

No higher value of a leads to a solution.
In fact suppose that $2 \leq a \leq b \leq c$.

Solving $abc = a + b + c$ for c gives $c = \frac{a+b}{ab-1}$.

For any fixed a we find that this solution achieves its greatest value when $b = a$; the values for $b = a, b = a + 1, b = a + 2$ go steadily down and the greatest value for c, namely $2a/(a^2 - 1)$, is never as big as a.
So no solution exists with $a \geq 2$.

The five-number case yields to a similar approach.

4 POWER CUTS

In fact you can make *any* whole number of feet of wire.

To see this we remark first of all that any whole number is of the form $3m$ (that is a multiple of 3) or $3m + 1$ (one more than a multiple of 3) or $3m + 2$ (two more than a multiple of 3).

Now the even powers of 2, that is $2^2 = 4, 2^4 = 16, 2^6 = 64$, etc., are all of the form $3m + 1$ (clearly multiplying a number $3m + 1$ by 4 produces a number of the form $3n + 1$), while the odd powers of 2, that is $2^1 = 2, 2^3 = 8, 2^5 = 32$, etc., are all of the form $3m + 2$ (again multiplying by 4 preserves the form of the number). So, in order to get $3m$ feet of wire, cut off m yards from a larger piece of wire, to get $3m + 1$ feet, cut enough yards off a larger *even* power of 2 feet, and to get $3m + 2$ feet, cut enough yards off a larger *odd* power of 2 feet.

There is a variant of this question involving calculators, as follows.
You are allowed to press in succession, in any order, and any number of times, the buttons 2, 3, ×, − and = on a calculator with a display of, say, 8 figures. Given a whole number N with up to 7 figures (one less than the display) can you make that number appear in the display? For numbers of the form $3m + 1$ and $3m + 2$ we can follow the procedure of the answer above: first use $2 \times 2 \times \ldots$ to get the next even or odd power of 2 above N, and then $- 3 - 3 - 3 \ldots$ to come down to N. (There may be much quicker ways, of course. For example, 22 could be obtained by pressing '2' twice!)
For $N = 3m$ we can obtain $N + 2$ in this way and use -2 to come down to N.

A slightly harder problem to use the buttons 3, 4, ×, − and = to generate any given number.

5 SPADEWORK

(i) You start by playing the 7. I must play the 1. Then you play the 5 and I can't follow so you win. (Similarly 517 is a win if you start with the 5.)

(ii) If I start with an *even*-numbered card, you *can* force a win. The crucial point is that *whichever of us is forced to play the 1, loses*. (For his opponent plays the 7 or 5. These cannot already have been played since they have no other factor or multiple.)

It is helpful to draw a diagram in which numbers are linked if they can be played successively.

$\begin{array}{c}4\\1\\8\end{array}\!\!\!\searrow\!2-6-3-9-5-7$ (We don't draw the link of each number to 1.)

Suppose I start with 6. If you play 3, I'll play 9, forcing you to play 1.
So you play 2 (the only other choice); I play 4 and you play 8, or else I play 8 and you play 4. Either way I have to play 1, and lose.
So these games are 6248 and 6284 (in each case followed by 15 or 17).
An even length of game is a win for you.
If *I start with 2*, you play 6 and the game is 2639: a win for you.
If *I start with 4*, you play 8 and the game is 482639: a win for you.
If *I start with 8*, you play 4 and the game is 842639: a win for you.

I haven't a chance!

If the number of cards is either 40 or 100, there is a beautiful solution giving the first player a guaranteed win.

This game was developed at Juniper Green Junior School in Edinburgh.

6 CORNERED

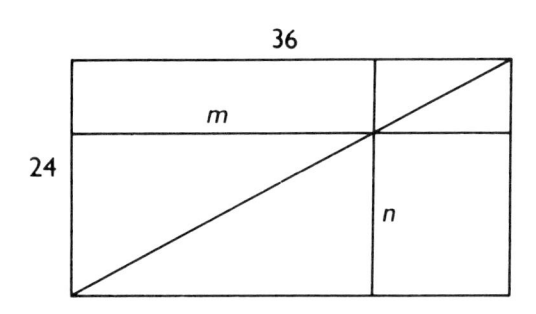

Whenever we have $\frac{24}{36} = \frac{n}{m}$ for whole numbers n and m, the diagonal will pass through the corner which is n cm above the base of the rectangle and m cm from the left-hand edge.
So we need to find all such whole numbers n and m.

Putting the fraction $\frac{24}{36}$ in its lowest terms, as $\frac{2}{3}$, gives us the smallest n and m.

Now $\frac{24}{36} = \frac{22}{33} = \frac{20}{30} = \frac{18}{27} = \frac{16}{24} = \frac{14}{21} = \frac{12}{18} = \frac{10}{15} = \frac{8}{12} = \frac{6}{9} = \frac{4}{6} = \frac{2}{3}$.

So the diagonal will go through these 12 corners and the bottom left, making *13 in all*.

Changing one dimension by 1 cm produces $\frac{25}{36}$ or $\frac{23}{36}$ or $\frac{24}{35}$ or $\frac{24}{37}$.

All these fractions are already in their lowest terms, so the diagonal goes through the bottom left and top right corners, and not through any others: that is through 2 corners only.

More generally with a $p \times q$ rectangle let $p = p_1 h$, $q = q_1 h$ where h is the highest common factor ($=$ greatest common divisor) of p and q.

Then $\frac{p}{q} = \frac{p_1}{q_1}$ and the fractions are $\frac{p_1}{q_1}, \frac{2p_1}{2q_1}, \ldots, \frac{hp_1}{hq_1}$, h in all.

Adding 1 for the bottom left-hand corner gives $h + 1$ corners.

Notice that another way of putting this is to say that the diagonal crosses $p + q - (p, q)$ squares, where (p, q) stands for the highest common factor h.

Suppose we have a solid $p \times q \times r$ block made up of 1 cm cubes and draw a diagonal line through the block.

How many of the cubes will this diagonal cross?

This time we have to allow for the diagonal passing through both corners and edges of cubes. The answer is

$$p + q + r - (p, q) - (q, r) - (p, r) + (p, q, r)$$

where as before brackets stand for highest common factors.

Thus for a $30 \times 70 \times 42$ block we get

$$142 - 10 - 14 - 6 + 2 = 114$$

cubes crossed by the diagonal.

7 GRINDING AWAY

Suppose that the first tooth of the smaller cog wheel which strikes the stone is the one marked A. Every time the big wheel turns round once a new tooth of the small wheel will be struck. So count round the small wheel 24 teeth from A, say clockwise, assuming the big wheel turns clockwise. This is the same as counting round $24 - 15 = 9$ teeth from A, and we arrive at B. A further 9 (or 24) teeth round in a clockwise direction gives C, then D, then E and then back to A. Thus *five teeth* are struck altogether.

You can also think of it this way:
The first time the two wheels are both in their original positions is after the big one has gone round 5 times and the small one 8 times.
(Then $5 \times 24 = 8 \times 15 = 120$ teeth of each will have passed through the point where the wheels engage. And 120 is the least number which is a multiple both of 24 and of 15.)
Every time the big wheel goes round once the stone strikes, so it strikes 5 times altogether.

Changing the numbers of teeth to 23 and 15 is the only way of making the stone strike all the teeth of the smaller wheel. With

24 and 16 it strikes 2 teeth
25 and 15 it strikes 3 teeth
24 and 14 it strikes 7 teeth.

The general formulae for wheels with p teeth and q teeth are as follows.
Let $[p, q]$ denote the least common multiple of p and q.
Then the stone strikes $[p, q]/p$ teeth of the second wheel.
Since $[p, q] = pq/(p, q)$ where (p, q) is the highest common factor (= greatest common divisor) of p and q the number of teeth struck by the stone can also be written $q/(p, q)$. This equals q (i.e. *all* teeth are struck) just when $(p, q) = 1$, that is when p and q have no common factor besides 1.
(Such p and q are called *co-prime*.)

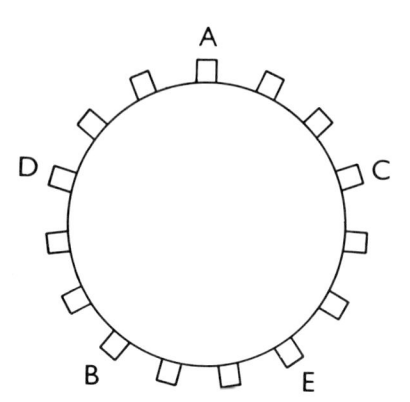

8 COUNTDOWN

Making a table gives the following:

Alison	Bill	Chris	Deductions from 18	Counters left
K	F	S	1 + 4 + 12	1
K	S	F	1 + 8 + 6	3
F	K	S	2 + 2 + 12	2
F	S	K	2 + 8 + 3	5
S	K	F	4 + 2 + 6	6
S	F	K	4 + 4 + 3	7

Since all the numbers in the right-hand column are different you can tell which child has which object.
If, for example, Alison, Bill and Chris are given 1, 3 and 4 counters respectively, then you *cannot* tell which child has which object. For instance, the allocations K, S, F and F, K, S give the same numbers left.

9 ARC LIGHT

The arc traced by Glim, or his remains, is like this:

The sharp points where he hits the ground are called 'cusps' and the ratio of the distance between two successive cusps to the height of the arches is equal to the ratio of the circumference of the wheel to its diameter, namely π, which is slightly less than $3\frac{1}{7}$. The curve is called the 'cycloid'. Note that the arches are not semicircles.

When Glim rides on some other point of the wheel he traces out a curve with the cusps smoothed out. Travelling on the flange of a train wheel produces loops.

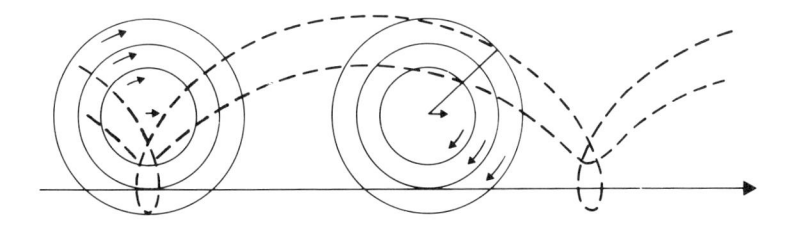

Of course with Glim at the centre he traces a straight line (but he still gets rather dizzy!).

10 MOWER TIME

Chris's method needs 9 turns, each of 180 degrees, totalling 45 seconds. On the other hand, Alex needs 16 turns of 90 degrees and 1 of 180 degrees, totalling 37 seconds. They both walk the same distance, so Alex wins. If they are to finish simultaneously, then
$9 \times$ Time for 180 degree turn $= 32 + 1 \times$ Time for 180 degree turn,
so the time for a 180 degree turn must be 4 seconds.

More generally, with a lawn a feet by b feet (where $a \geq b$ and a is the 'vertical dimension', that is 15 in the original problem), Chris needs $b - 1$ turns, all 180 degrees while Alex needs (provided $b > 1$!) $2b - 4$ turns of 90 degrees and 1 turn of 180 degrees. (See the upper diagram.) So Chris takes $5(b - 1)$ seconds and Alex takes $2(2b - 4) + 5$ seconds, which is always shorter (unless $b = 1$ or $b = 2$ in which case the two methods are identical!).

Writing q for the time for a quarter-turn and h the time for a half-turn, the times are $h(b - 1)$ and $q(b - 4) + h$, and these are equal precisely when $h = 2q$ (or $b = 2$). So thus far the answers are the same as before.

But if $a < b$ the situation is completely different, for while Chris still needs $b - 1$ turns of 180 degrees, taking $(b - 1)h$ seconds, now Alex needs $2a - 3$ turns of 90 degrees and 1 turn of 180 degrees, taking a total of $(2a - 3)q + h$ seconds. (See the lower diagram.)
So now we get equality when $(2a - 3)q = (b - 2)h$, which depends on the dimensions of the lawns.

When $a = 10$ and $b = 15$, with $q = 2$ (the values we started with, but with a now the shorter side), the condition for equality of time taken by the two methods becomes $h = \frac{34}{13} = 2.62$ seconds.

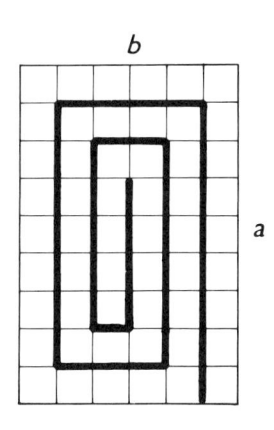

$a \geq b$: $2b - 4$ quarter turns

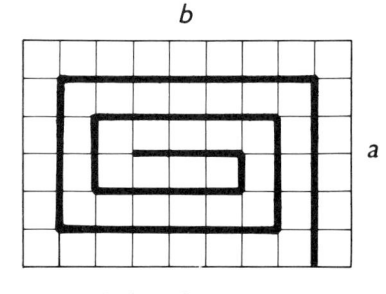

$a < b$: $2a - 3$ quarter turns

11 SLIPPED DISC

It depends on which direction you move half of the record.
Keeping the left-hand half fixed and moving the right-hand half, you find:

Moving up by 1 groove: single clockwise spiral
Moving down by 1 groove: 3 anticlockwise spirals
Moving up by 2 grooves: 3 clockwise spirals
Moving down by 2 grooves: 5 anticlockwise spirals.

Further displacements continue the pattern.

12 CIRCLE LINE

To satisfy the conditions of the problem the stations must be evenly placed round the circle, so that each is the same (shorter) distance round the circle from the other two. In the diagram M is the main station and A and B the two suburban stations.

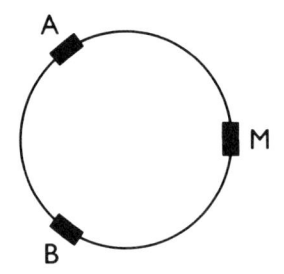

13 NEW CIRCLE LINE

It is *not* correct to have M, A, B and C evenly spaced round the circle. For then if one goes from M to B, and then as far again, one comes back to M and not to one of the other two stations.

One solution to the problem is to place two of the suburban stations, as before in Problem 12, equidistant from the main station and from each other, and then to place the third station half-way from the main station to either of these two. A more subtle solution is to place A one seventh of the way round from M, one way or the other, B two sevenths of the way round and C four sevenths of the way round. These are the only possibilities, apart from permuting the names A, B and C.

To see this let A be the first station that we reach if we travel round the circle anticlockwise from M, at a distance d from M, say, and let B be the station that is at a distance $2d$ anticlockwise round the track from M. Then if we go a distance $4d$ from M we must come either to A again or to C.

In the first case it must be that $3d$ takes us all the way round the circle back to M. That is, we must have M, A and B as in Problem 12, and the only possible position for C is half-way from M to B clockwise, for we agreed at the outset that A was the first station reached if we travelled anticlockwise from M.

In the second case C is reached at a distance $4d$ from M.
Then at a distance $8d$ from M we must come either to A or to B.

If $8d$ takes us to A then $7d$ must take us all the way round the circle a whole number of times, and d must be so many sevenths of the full circle.
If A is one-seventh of the way round anticlockwise, then B is two-sevenths of the way round and C is four-sevenths of the way round, or equivalently three-sevenths of the way round clockwise. If A is two-sevenths of the way round anticlockwise then B is four-sevenths of the way round and C eight-sevenths, or equivalently one-seventh of the way round, not the case as we supposed that A was the first station reached.
If A is three-sevenths of the way round then B is six-sevenths of the way round and C twelve-sevenths, or equivalently five-sevenths of the way round. This covers all possibilities.

On the other hand if $8d$ takes us to B then $6d$ must take us all the way round the circle a whole number of times, and d must be so many sixths of the full circle. Clearly the only possibility is that A is one-sixth of the way round anticlockwise, with B two-sixths, that is one-third, of the way round and C four-sixths, that is two-thirds, of the way round.

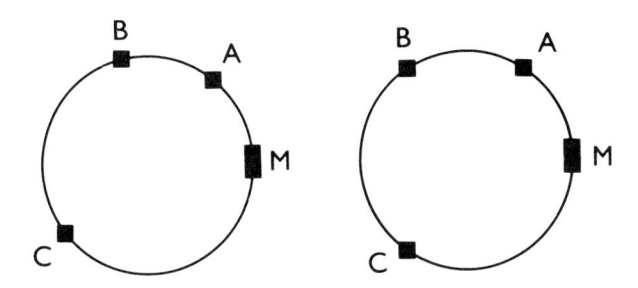

It is quite interesting to extend this question further.
What we have just found is the existence of one 'cycle of order two' and two 'cycles of order three' on the circle, under the operation of doubling the distance from the main station, or base point M.
How many cycles are there of orders 4, 5, 6, ...?
Alternatively we could look for cycles of various orders under the operation of trebling the distance from M.
There is plenty of scope for further research!

14 LET'S FACE IT

There are 15 different tetrahedra that can be made from four equilateral triangles chosen from three colours and, in fact, 36 that can be made from four colours. Many give 34 as the answer, missing out the very special case where just one triangle of each of the four colours is used.

In fact in this last case, and in this case only, *two distinct* tetrahedra can be made, one of which is the mirror image of the other, making 36, as we said, and not 35 in all. You may be interested in the formula underlying these results.

It is well known that the number of ways of choosing k things from n possibilities, when repetitions are not allowed, is

$$\binom{n}{k} = \frac{n(n-1)(n-2)\ldots(n-k+1)}{1.2.3.\ldots k}.$$

It is not so well known that, when repetitions are allowed, the number is

$$\binom{n+k-1}{k} = \frac{n(n+1)(n+2)\ldots(n+k-1)}{1.2.3.\ldots k}$$

Here, when the four sides have to be painted with colours chosen from three, $n = 3$ and $k = 4$, so the number of ways is

$$\frac{3.4.5.6}{1.2.3.4} = 15,$$

while, when four colours are available, $n = 4$ and $k = 4$, and the number of ways (orientation apart) is

$$\frac{4.5.6.7}{1.2.3.4} = 35.$$

Of course, with numbers as small as these, and a weekend to do the work, it is not difficult to make complete lists of the possibilities!

15 VALHALLA

Whoever makes the second move can win.
For example suppose Val plays first. She has essentially 3 choices, as shown in the diagrams.

Hal then puts his piece across the squares marked x, leaving Val with only one possible move and still allowing Hal to reply.
If Hal plays first there is similarly a clinching move by Val.

We leave you to look at differently shaped boards.
An easily made Valhalla set consists of a 4×4 (or larger) board, several black 1×1 squares of plywood and a supply of white 1×2 rectangles.
At the outset each player has several white pieces, several squares of the board having been blocked off with black pieces.
In the example six squares have been so blocked off.
One player has the option of whether to play vertically as Val or horizontally as Hal, while the other has the option of whether to play first or second.
With a little experimentation you will discover that with careful play certain boards should be winnable by Val, others by Hal, others by whoever plays first and yet others by whoever plays second.

'Valhalla' is originally due to Göran Andersson and called by Martin Gardner 'Crosscram'. There is an extensive theory of the game due to Professor John Conway who calls it 'Domineering'. For details see *On Numbers and Games* by J. H. Conway, Academic Press, 1976, pages 74–75 and 114–121, and *Winning Ways* Vol. I by E. R. Berlekamp, J. H. Conway and R. K. Guy, Academic Press, 1982, Chapter 5.

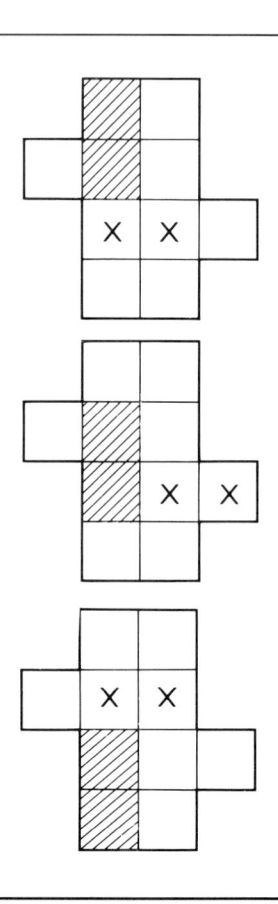

16 DAMP COURSE

The boy can escape. He works his way slowly from the centre to half-way to the circumference, making sure that one bucket is as far to his left as another is to his right, the third being directly behind him. This he can do, as he can keep pace with any movements that the buckets make, as they have twice as far to go as he needs to go to keep up with them.

Once half-way he then makes a dash for it and just manages to get through, as he has half the radius to run while the bucket to either side has slightly more than the radius to travel.

This is because π, the ratio of the circumference of any circle to its diameter, is approximately equal to $22/7$, which is a little bit greater than 3, from which it follows that the ratio of the circumference to the radius is a little bit greater than 6. Thus the distance between two of the buckets, measured round the circle, is somewhat greater than twice the radius.

17 NIGHT AT THE ROUND TABLE

Obviously you have to go between two of the nasties, but then the total distance from yourself to these two *round the edge of the table* does not depend on where you are, and the distance to the third will be greatest when you are directly opposite it. So the thing to do is to go between the two that are furthest apart from each other and then sit directly opposite the third. This position is unique if the nasties are irregularly spaced.

Note that for three points on a circle it does not make sense to speak of the 'middle' one.

18 FEARSOME FOURSOME

Let the nasties be at points A, B, C and D and let the points directly opposite these be A*, B*, C* and D*. If these points are all distinct then there is one and only one arc between two nasties containing either *two* or *four* of the opposite points.

(To see this put A and A* on the circle first, then consider in succession the possible places for B and B*, C and C* and D and D*, at least as far as their order round the circle is concerned).

In the first case *anywhere* between these two opposite points and in the second case *anywhere* between the middle two of them will do.

The arc in which these opposite points lie needn't be the largest arc. Look, for example, at the case when the four nasties are at 10 o'clock, 11 o'clock, 3 o'clock and 6 o'clock.

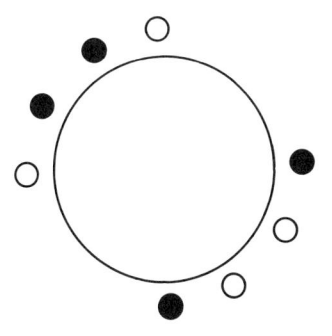

To round things off one should then consider the cases where either one or two pairs of nasties are exactly opposite each other. For instance, if A and B are opposite and reading round the table gives ACD*BC*D, you find that anywhere on the arc C*D*, *including the point* B, gives the minimum distance. Surely the nastiest case!

19 SPACE MEN

The only two space men that can fit into a cubical space capsule two centimetres each way are the ones we have called Sirius and Pluto in Problem 20.
It is sometimes difficult to recognise Sirius when he is lying on one side or another, but these two possibilities really are the only ones.

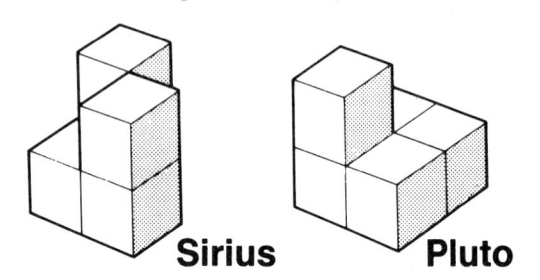

Sirius   **Pluto**

20 GEMINI

Let A denote a single cube on the ground, B a cube one centimetre above the ground and C two cubes, one on top of the other.
Then there are five spacemen who are indistinguishable from their mirror images, namely:

$$\frac{AC}{C}(Sirius) \quad \frac{CA}{AA}(Pluto) \quad \frac{CAA}{A} \quad \frac{ACA}{A} \quad \text{and} \quad \frac{AAA}{C},$$

and there are twelve others consisting of *six pairs of twins*, namely:

$$\frac{AA}{BC}(Castor) \quad \frac{AAA}{C} \quad \frac{ACA}{A} \quad \frac{CAA}{B} \quad \frac{AA}{CA} \quad \text{and} \quad \frac{AA}{AC},$$

together with their mirror images, making *seventeen* in all.